GoodFood magazine

101 TEMPTING DESSERTS

Published by BBC Books
BBC Worldwide Limited
80 Wood Lane
London W12 0TT

First published 2006
Copyright © BBC Worldwide 2006
All photographs © *BBC Good Food Magazine* 2006

All the recipes contained in this book first appeared in *BBC Good Food Magazine*.

ISBN 0 563 52292 5

Commissioning Editor: Vivien Bowler
Project Editor: Sarah Reece
Designer: Kathryn Gammon
Production Controller: Peter Hunt

Set in Bookman Old Style and Helvetica
Printed and bound in Italy by LEGO SpA
Colour origination by Dot Gradations Ltd, UK

GoodFood
magazine

101 TEMPTING DESSERTS
TRIED-AND-TESTED RECIPES

Editor
Angela Nilsen

BBC
BOOKS

Contents

Introduction

It is hard not to be tempted by a luscious dessert at the end of a meal, and at *BBC Good Food Magazine* we have always been proud of the amazing creations we have devised to suit all types of tastes and occasions. For this special collection, we have gathered together some of our favourites, from cheesecakes, exotic fruit salads and pavlovas, to ice cream sundaes and chocolate mousses.

Even if you think you don't have time to make desserts, just flick through this book for inspiration and you will find creamy creations that can be put together in a matter of minutes, puddings that you would never guess are low fat, including *Creamy Saffron Yogurt*, pictured opposite (see page 200 for the recipe), as well as seasonal tarts that are easy to make yet elegant enough for entertaining.

To ensure simplicity and practicality, all the recipes have been thoroughly tested by the Good Food team, plus each one has its own nutritional breakdown – which means you get to choose just how indulgent you want to be.

Angela Nilsen

Angela Nilsen
BBC Good Food Magazine

Conversion tables

NOTES ON THE RECIPES
• Eggs are medium in the UK and Australia (large in America) unless stated otherwise.
• Wash all fresh produce before preparation.

OVEN TEMPERATURES

Gas	°C	Fan °C	°F	Oven temp.
¼	110	90	225	Very cool
½	120	100	250	Very cool
1	140	120	275	Cool or slow
2	150	130	300	Cool or slow
3	160	140	325	Warm
4	180	160	350	Moderate
5	190	170	375	Moderately hot
6	200	180	400	Fairly hot
7	220	200	425	Hot
8	230	210	450	Very hot
9	240	220	475	Very hot

APPROXIMATE WEIGHT CONVERSIONS
• All the recipes in this book list both imperial and metric measurements. Conversions are approximate and have been rounded up or down. Follow one set of measurements only; do not mix the two.
• Cup measurements, which are used by cooks in Australia and America, have not been listed here as they vary from ingredient to ingredient. Please use kitchen scales to measure dry/solid ingredients.

SPOON MEASURES

• Spoon measurements are level unless otherwise specified.

• 1 teaspoon = 5ml

• 1 tablespoon = 15ml

• 1 Australian tablespoon = 20ml (cooks in Australia should measure 3 teaspoons where 1 tablespoon is specified in a recipe)

APPROXIMATE LIQUID CONVERSIONS

metric	imperial	AUS	US
50ml	2fl oz	¼ cup	¼ cup
125ml	4fl oz	½ cup	½ cup
175ml	6fl oz	¾ cup	¾ cup
225ml	8fl oz	1 cup	1 cup
300ml	10fl oz/½ pint	½ pint	1¼ cups
450ml	16fl oz	2 cups	2 cups/1 pint
600ml	20fl oz/1 pint	1 pint	2½ cups
1 litre	35fl oz/1¾ pints	1¾ pints	1 quart

You can sprinkle crushed gingernut biscuits between the layers
if you want more of a crunch.

Blackberry Honey Creams

500g tub Greek yogurt
2–3 tbsp runny honey
300g/10oz blackberries
225g bottle fruit coulis (widely
available)

Takes 5 minutes • Serves 4

1 Beat the yogurt with honey to taste.
2 Divide half the berries between four glasses, drizzle with some coulis and spoon the yogurt over.
3 Top with the remaining berries and some coulis. Serve immediately with the rest of the coulis.

• Per serving 242 kcalories, protein 9g, carbohydrate 27g, fat 12g, saturated fat 7.1g, fibre 3.2g, added sugar 15.9g, salt 0.23g

The sugar dissolves into the cream during chilling
to make a lovely syrupy topping.

Cheat's Berry Brûlée

425ml/¾ pint double cream
400g tub Greek yogurt
4 tbsp light muscovado sugar

TO SERVE
100g bag pecan nuts
4 tsp clear honey
125g punnet blueberries
125g punnet raspberries (or
use frozen)
icing sugar, for dusting (optional)

Takes 20 minutes, plus chilling •
Serves 6

1 In a large bowl, lightly whip the double cream until soft and billowy. Fold in the yogurt, then spoon into a shallow serving dish and smooth the surface with the back of the spoon. Scatter the sugar over the top, cover and chill in the fridge for 2–3 hours or overnight.

2 Dry fry the the pecans in a frying pan, stirring frequently to prevent them from burning, until lightly toasted. Add the honey, stir well and quickly remove from the heat.

3 Tip the hot nuts and honey over the chilled cream and scatter over the berries. If you prefer a showy effect, dust with icing sugar. Serve straight away.

• Per serving 570 kcalories, protein 7g, carbohydrate 20g, fat 52g, saturated fat 25g, fibre 2g, added sugar 13g, salt 0.19g

A quick way of turning a tub of ice cream
into an indulgent treat.

Cappucino Tiramisu

8 sponge fingers
cold coffee
142ml carton double cream
1 tbsp icing sugar
3 tbsp Baileys
8 scoops Baileys ice cream
1 chocolate flake

Takes 10 minutes • Serves 4

1 Halve the sponge fingers and press them into four glasses. Pour over enough cold coffee to soak the sponge. Whisk the cream with the icing sugar and the Baileys until it goes into soft peaks.
2 Spoon the ice cream into each glass, then top with the whipped cream.
3 Break up the chocolate flake and scatter over the cream.

• Per serving 566 kcalories, protein 7g, carbohydrate 40g, fat 42g, saturated fat 22.8g, fibre 0.2g, added sugar 30g, salt 0.27g

This is a great idea for using frozen berries. And it's so quick you can whip it up in an instant if you have unexpected guests.

Iced Berries with Hot-choc Sauce

500g/1lb 2oz mixed frozen berries
(blackberries, blueberries,
raspberries, redcurrants)

FOR THE SAUCE
142ml carton double cream
140g/5oz white chocolate
1 tbsp white rum (optional)

Takes 10 minutes • Serves 4

1 Make the sauce. Pour the cream into a small saucepan and break in the chocolate. Heat gently, stirring, until the chocolate melts into a smooth sauce. Take care not to overheat or the chocolate will seize into a hard lump.
2 Remove from the heat and stir in the rum, if using. Scatter the frozen berries on four dessert plates or in shallow bowls.
3 Pour the hot chocolate sauce over the fruits and serve immediately, as the fruits start to defrost.

• Per serving 377 kcalories, protein 5g, carbohydrate 28g, fat 28g, saturated fat 11g, fibre 3g, added sugar 17g, salt 0.14g

This is an excellent cheat's recipe as there's no cooking involved, it makes the most of ready-made cake and sauces, and looks spectacular.

Banoffi Trifles

6 tbsp tropical fruit juice
(from a carton)
2 tbsp rum or brandy
2 firm bananas
8 thin slices from a bought
Madeira cake
2 tbsp Belgian chocolate sauce
4 heaped tbsp *dulce de leche*,
or other toffee sauce
225g tub mascarpone
250ml/9fl oz chilled custard
(from a tub)
a block of dark chocolate (any type
or size will do)

Takes 15 minutes • Serves 4

1 In a large bowl, stir the tropical fruit juice with the rum or brandy. Slice the bananas into the fruit juice mixture and toss together. Sandwich the slices of Madeira cake with the chocolate sauce, dice it into squares and pile in the bottom of four pretty glasses.
2 Top with the bananas and rum mixture then add a heaped spoonful of dulce de leche to make another layer. Next, beat the mascarpone and custard together until smooth, then spoon on top of the mixture.
3 Chill for up to 2 hours until ready to serve. Before serving, run a potato peeler down the flat back of the bar of chocolate to make shavings and scatter indulgently on top of the trifles.

• Per serving 787 kcalories, protein 9g, carbohydrate 87g, fat 46g, saturated fat 25.1g, fibre 1.6g, added sugar 50.2g, salt 0.82g

You can get the clementines ready before the meal.
Simply reheat them gently just before serving.

Hot Clementines with Brandy Sauce

25g/1oz butter
2 tbsp light muscovado sugar
150ml/¼ pint smooth orange juice
from a carton
6 clementines, peeled and halved
horizontally
3 tbsp brandy
good-quality vanilla ice cream and
thin, crisp biscuits, to serve

Takes 20 minutes • Serves 4

1 Melt the butter in a heavy-based frying pan, sprinkle in the sugar and stir well until dissolved, then pour in the orange juice and boil for 2–3 minutes until beginning to go syrupy.

2 Add the clementines and brandy and boil for 3–5 minutes, spooning the sauce over until it is really syrupy.

3 To serve, put three clementine halves on four dessert plates, spoon the sauce over and finish with a scoop of ice cream and a biscuit. Serve at once.

• Per serving 142 kcalories, protein 1g, carbohydrate 17g, fat 5g, saturated fat 3g, fibre 1g, added sugar 6g, salt 0.14g

The combination of hot caramelised sauce and still-chilly fruits
is irresistible in this simple, yet sophisticated dessert.

Gratin of Summer Berries

140g/5oz strawberries, hulled and
cut into halves or quarters
140g/5oz each fresh raspberries and
blueberries
finely grated zest of 1 small lemon
100g/4oz white chocolate
142ml carton double cream
2 tbsp icing sugar

Takes 15 minutes, plus cooling •
Serves 4

1 Scatter the berries between four medium
ramekins or one large, shallow heatproof dish,
preferably in a single layer. Sprinkle with the
lemon zest, cover and chill until ready to serve.
2 Meanwhile, break up the chocolate into
a small heatproof bowl. Heat the cream in a
small pan until almost boiling, then pour onto
the chocolate. Leave for 3 minutes, then stir
slowly until dissolved. Allow to cool to room
temperature until thickened.
3 To serve, heat the grill for a good 5 minutes
until glowing hot. Spoon the chocolate cream
over the berries, sprinkle over the icing sugar
and grill for 2–3 minutes, until the sauce
begins to brown, turning the dish if necessary.
Remove and serve immediately.

• Per serving 356 kcalories, protein 3g, carbohydrate
27g, fat 27g, saturated fat 11g, fibre 1g, added sugar
20g, salt 0.10g

The flavour of this velvety pud is best when freshly made, but it will keep for up to a month in the freezer.

Almost-instant Wine Ice Cream

150ml sweet white wine, such as
Orange Muscat and Flora,
plus a little extra to serve
3 rounded tbsp golden caster sugar
284ml carton double cream
summer fruits, such as blackberries,
raspberries and redcurrants,
to serve

Takes 10 minutes, plus freezing •
Serves 4–6

1 Tip the wine and sugar into a bowl and whisk together. Gradually whisk in the cream until it starts to thicken and just hold its shape.

2 Pour into a rigid container and freeze until firm, about 3–4 hours.

3 Serve in scoops with seasonal summer fruits splashed with a little more sweet wine.

• Per serving for four 461 kcalories, protein 1g, carbohydrate 23g, fat 38g, saturated fat 21.4g, fibre none, added sugar 19.7g, salt 0.05g

Spoil yourself with this indulgent Italian treat. You can use a mixture of nuts instead of the almonds.

Cherry Cream Sundaes

284ml carton double cream
2 tbsp icing sugar
200g/8oz toasted almonds or hazelnuts, chopped
2–3 tbsp dark rum
10 amaretti biscuits
10 canned cherries (or fresh when in season)
50g/2oz dark chocolate, melted, to drizzle

Takes 20 minutes • Makes 10

1 Arrange ten paper muffin cases on a baking sheet. Whisk together the cream and icing sugar until stiff. Fold in the almonds or hazelnuts, and the rum.
2 Crumble the biscuits and put the pieces in the bottom of the paper cases. Divide the cream between them and top with a cherry.
3 Freeze for 1–2 hours until firm. (They will keep in the freezer for up to 2 weeks.) Remove from the freezer 20 minutes before serving, and drizzle with the chocolate.

• Per sundae 329 kcalories, protein 5g, carbohydrate 16g, fat 27g, saturated fat 10g, fibre 2g, added sugar 8g, salt 0.11g

If you have a glut of fruit, make a large batch of compote and freeze in usable quantities. It's great hot or cold as a pancake filling.

Quick Summer Compote

500g/1lb 2oz mixed berries
(blackcurrants, blueberries,
raspberries, redcurrants,
strawberries)
50–85g/2–3oz golden caster sugar
ice cream, to serve

FLAVOURINGS TO CHOOSE FROM
1 vanilla pod
1 cinnamon stick
2–3 sprigs of fresh mint or
lemon balm

Takes 15 minutes • Serves 4

1 If using strawberries, hull, halve or quarter to make them a similar size to the other berries. Tip all the fruits into a large pan with 2–3 tablespoons water, sugar to taste and your choice of flavourings.
2 Bring to the boil, then simmer for 3–5 minutes. Don't overcook, or the fruits will not hold their shape.
3 Serve hot or chilled with scoops of ice cream. This keeps in the fridge for up to 2 days, or in the freezer for up to 3 months.

• Per serving 83 kcalories, protein 1g, carbohydrate 20g, fat none, saturated fat none, fibre 3g, added sugar 13g, salt 0.01g

For a tropical version, scoop the seeds and juice
from 2 ripe passion fruit into the syrup.

Raspberry and Mango Salad

200ml/7fl oz cranberry juice
1 tbsp caster sugar
1 large ripe mango
150g punnet raspberries
a dash of vodka, optional
vanilla ice cream or yogurt, to serve

Takes 10 minutes • Serves 4

1 In a small pan, bring the cranberry juice
and sugar to a rolling boil, then remove from
the heat and leave to cool.
2 Meanwhile, peel and thinly slice the
mango, then tip into a large bowl with the
raspberries.
3 Add a dash of vodka to the syrup, if
using, then pour the cranberry syrup over
the fruit and spoon into bowls. Serve with
scoops of ice cream or spoonfuls of yogurt.

• Per serving 106 kcalories, protein 1g, carbohydrate
27g, fat 1g, saturated fat none, fibre 3g, added sugar
11g, salt 0.02g

If you can't find Scotch pancakes, French-style crêpes would work equally well. Look out for ready-made ones in your local supermarket.

Cherry Pancakes

12 bought Scotch pancakes
bottled cherries in kirsch or brandy
(or canned cherries in syrup),
to serve
crème fraîche or whipped cream,
to serve

Takes 10 minutes • Serves 4

1 Warm the pancakes through briefly in the microwave.
2 Tip the cherries into a pan and warm through gently (or warm in the microwave).
3 Spoon the cherries and their juices over the pancakes and top with a big dollop of crème fraîche or cream.

• Per serving 243 kcalories, protein 5g, carbohydrate 39g, fat 9g, saturated fat 2.2g, fibre 1.4g, added sugar 5.1g, salt 0.96g

These chocolate mousses are mild and fudgy so children will love them, too. Put the mousse in one large bowl for everyone to dive into.

Mars Bar Mousses

4 standard (65g) Mars bars, chopped into pieces
50ml/2fl oz milk
4 tbsp cocoa powder
3 large egg whites
chocolate shavings, to decorate

Takes 20–25 minutes, plus setting • Serves 6

1 Put the Mars bars, milk and cocoa in a heavy-based saucepan. Cook over a very gentle heat, stirring constantly, until the chocolate has melted. Transfer to a bowl and leave to cool for 15 minutes, whisking frequently with a wire whisk to blend in any pieces of fudge that rise to the surface, to leave a smooth mixture.
2 Whisk the egg whites in a separate bowl to soft peaks. Using a metal spoon, fold a quarter of the whites into the chocolate sauce to lighten it, then fold in the remainder.
3 Turn the mixture into six small cups, glasses or ramekins and chill in the fridge to set, for at least 2 hours, before serving. Serve topped with chocolate shavings.

• Per serving 369 kcalories, protein 8g, carbohydrate 50g, fat 17g, saturated fat 9g, fibre 1g, added sugar 39g, salt 0.60g.

The perfect, speedy no-cook treat for a get-together. Simply melt, mix and stick in the fridge.

Quick Chocolate-nut Slice

100g/4oz butter
400g/14oz dark chocolate, broken in pieces
50g/2oz golden caster sugar
½ tsp ground cinnamon
200g/8oz macaroons or coconut biscuits, broken into pieces
100g/4oz Brazil nuts, roughly chopped
desiccated coconut, to serve
fresh fruit or ice cream, to serve (optional)

Takes 20 minutes, plus chilling • Serves 6

1 Line a 900g/2lb loaf tin with a double layer of cling film. Melt the butter, chocolate and sugar in the microwave on Medium for 2–3 minutes, or in a bowl set over a pan of simmering water over a low heat. Stir in the cinnamon, macaroons or coconut biscuits, and the nuts.

2 Pour the mixture into the prepared tin, smooth over the surface with a knife and cover completely with cling film. Leave in the fridge to set for at least 2 hours.

3 To serve, turn out onto a plate, remove the cling film and sprinkle with desiccated coconut. This dessert is fairly rich, so slice into thin pieces. Serve with fresh fruit or ice cream if you like.

• Per serving 759 kcalories, protein 9g, carbohydrate 73g, fat 50g, saturated fat 22g, fibre 3g, added sugar 70g, salt 0.32g

A clever and easy last-minute dessert that is
wonderful served with coffee.

Amaretti Biscuits with Ice Cream

24 soft amaretti biscuits
good quality vanilla ice cream
amaretto liqueur (optional)

Takes 10 minutes • Serves 6

1 Sandwich a small scoop of ice cream
between two amaretti biscuits.
2 Put two filled biscuits on each plate.
3 Serve drizzled with a little amaretto,
if you wish.

• Per serving 262 kcalories, protein 4g, carbohydrate
46g, fat 7g, saturated fat 4g, fibre 1g, added sugar
17g, salt 0.49g

This speedy dessert makes the
perfect end to a spicy meal.

Marvellous Mangoes

3 mangoes
3 tbsp Cointreau
handful of fresh mint leaves,
shredded

Takes 10 minutes • Serves 6

1 Peel the mangoes and carefully slice off each fleshy side close to the stone. Slice the mango flesh.
2 Splash with the Cointreau, then cover and chill for at least 2 hours (or overnight).
3 Serve straight from the fridge, showered with the shredded mint leaves.

• Per serving 81 kcalories, protein 1g, carbohydrate 16g, fat none, saturated fat none, fibre 3g, added sugar 2g, salt 0.01g

A pretty, summery idea that looks like 2 hours' work,
but only takes 15 minutes!

Lemon Cheesecake Tartlets

4 tbsp lemon curd
2 × 200g tubs Philadelphia lite
cheese
6 tbsp summer fruit sauce, from
a bottle
8 sweet dessert tartlet cases (from
a pack)
100g/4oz blueberries
100g/4oz raspberries
1 tbsp cassis (blackcurrant liqueur)
icing sugar, for dusting
fresh mint sprigs

Takes 15 minutes • Serves 4

1 Beat the lemon curd into the soft cheese until smooth and creamy. Pour 1 teaspoon of summer fruit sauce into each dessert tartlet, then top with a spoonful of the cheese mixture (set aside the remainder).
2 Carefully mix the berries together, then pile onto the cheese mixture. Stir the cassis into the remaining sauce. (You can make the tarts and sauce up to this stage and chill for 2–3 hours.)
3 Dust the tartlets with icing sugar. Drizzle lines of the sauce over half of four dinner plates with a teaspoon and spoon the remaining cheesecake mixture in the centre. Put two tarts on each plate, propping one of the tarts against the cheesecake mixture. Add a sprig of mint for an extra flourish.

• Per serving 599 kcalories, protein 14g, carbohydrate 58g, fat 35g, saturated fat 12.9g, fibre 2.8g, added sugar 13.3g, salt 1.76g

This is a traditional American recipe that you're bound to love. But it's probably best kept to the occasional treat with all those calories!

Pumpkin Pie

500g pack ready-made shortcrust pastry
2 large eggs
2 egg yolks
284ml carton double cream
425g can 100% pure pumpkin
397g can condensed milk
1 tsp each ground cinnamon, ginger and nutmeg

FOR THE TOPPING
50g/2oz pecan or walnut pieces, coarsely chopped
85g/3oz light muscovado sugar
50g/2oz butter, melted

TO SERVE
142ml carton double cream

Takes 1 hour 20 minutes, plus cooling • Serves 8

1 Preheat the oven to 200°C/Gas 6/fan oven 180°C. Roll out the pastry and use to line a 23cm/9in rimmed pie dish, 5cm/2in deep. Trim and scallop the edge. Chill for 30 minutes. Prick the pastry base, then bake blind for 12 minutes. Remove, and set aside. Lower the oven to 180°C/Gas 4/fan oven 160°C.
2 To make the filling, whisk the eggs and yolks until frothy. Add 250ml/9fl oz of the cream, then the other filling ingredients. Whisk thoroughly. Pour into the pie, bake for 50 minutes or until just set. Cool for 2 hours.
3 Preheat the grill to high. Mix the topping ingredients and spoon over the pie. Protect the pastry edge with strips of foil, then grill about 12cm/4½in from the heat, for 2–3 minutes, until bubbling. Remove and cool. Whip all the remaining cream and serve with the pie.

• Per serving 681 kcalories, protein 10g, carbohydrate 49g, fat 51g, saturated fat 25g, fibre 2g, added sugar 11g, salt 1.11g

This is a great mix of two classic rhubarb puds. It's particularly good served warm with chilled crème fraîche or single cream.

Rhubarb and Custard Pie

350g/12oz rhubarb, cut into bite-sized pieces
100g/4oz golden caster sugar
350g/12oz sweet shortcrust pastry
1 large egg and 1 egg yolk
1 tsp vanilla extract
1 tbsp plain flour
284ml carton single cream

FOR THE TOPPING
50g/2oz butter, melted
50g/2oz demerara sugar
50g/2oz porridge oats
½ tsp ground ginger

Takes 1¾–2 hours • Serves 8

1 Put the rhubarb in a frying pan with half the sugar. Warm until the sugar dissolves. Tip into a bowl and cool. Preheat the oven to 180°C/Gas 4/fan oven 160°C. Roll the pastry quite thinly and line a deep, loose-based 24cm/9½in fluted flan tin. Bake blind for 20 minutes until the pastry is pale golden.
2 Beat together the egg and egg yolk, vanilla extract, remaining caster sugar and flour. Gradually whisk in the cream with a spoonful or two of juice from the rhubarb. Spoon the rhubarb into the pastry case and pour the cream mixture over. Turn the oven up to 200°C/Gas 6/fan oven 180°C and bake for 20 minutes, or until the custard is lightly set.
3 Mix the topping ingredients and spoon over. Return the pie to the oven for 15 minutes until the top is golden and the custard just set.

• Per serving 456 kcalories, protein 6g, carbohydrate 49g, fat 28g, saturated fat 13g, fibre 2g, added sugar 24g, salt 0.43g

Vanilla sugar is widely used in France to give a subtle flavour to baking and desserts. You'll find it with the baking ingredients in supermarkets.

Flat Apple and Vanilla Tart

375g pack puff pastry, preferably all-butter
5 large eating apples – Cox's, russets or Elstar
juice of 1 lemon
25g/1oz butter, cut into small pieces
3 tsp vanilla sugar or 1 tsp vanilla extract
1 tbsp caster sugar
3 rounded tbsp apricot conserve
vanilla ice cream or crème fraîche, to serve

Takes 25–30 minutes • Serves 6

1 Preheat the oven to 220ºC/Gas 7/fan oven 200ºC. Roll out the pastry and trim to a round about 35cm/14in across. Transfer to a baking sheet lined with parchment paper.
2 Peel, core and thinly slice the apples and toss in the lemon juice. Spread over the pastry to within 2cm/¾in of the edges. Curl up the edges slightly to stop the juices running off.
3 Dot the top with the butter and sprinkle with vanilla and caster sugar. Bake for 15–20 minutes until the apples are tender and the pastry crisp.
4 Warm the conserve (you can sieve it if you like) and brush over the apples and pastry edge. Serve hot with vanilla ice cream or crème fraîche.

• Per serving 356 kcalories, protein 4g, carbohydrate 47g, fat 18g, saturated fat 8g, fibre 2g, added sugar 10.7g, salt 0.58g

You can prepare this melt-in-the-mouth pud in the morning
or afternoon before you intend to serve it.

Limoncello Plum Tart

500g pack ready-made shortcrust pastry
zest and juice of 2 unwaxed lemons
4 tbsp double cream
100g pack ground almonds
200g/8oz golden caster sugar
5 eggs
100g/4oz butter, melted
8 tbsp limoncello liqueur
6 plums, stoned and cut into wedges
icing sugar, to serve

Takes 1–1¼ hours • Serves 12

1 Roll out the pastry and use to line a loose-bottomed tart tin, 25cm/10in in diameter and about 3–4cm/1¼–1½in deep. Chill for at least 30 minutes.

2 Preheat the oven to 180°C/Gas 4/fan oven 160°C. Line the pastry with foil, fill with baking beans and bake blind for 15 minutes. Remove beans and foil.

3 Put the lemon zest and juice, cream, almonds, sugar, eggs and melted butter in a large bowl and whisk until smooth, then stir in the limoncello. Put the plums in the pastry case, then pour the custard mixture over. Bake for about 20–30 minutes until the custard is just set. Allow to cool, then dredge with icing sugar before serving.

• Per slice 924 kcalories, protein 14g, carbohydrate 83g, fat 57g, saturated fat 25g, fibre 4g, added sugar 38g, salt 0.86g

Enjoy this cheat's version of the tarts seen in pâtisserie shops all over southwest France during the nectarine season.

Caramelised Nectarine Tart

400g/14oz puff pastry
50g/2oz butter
juice of ½ lemon
50g/2oz soft toffees, such as Werther's Original
4 ripe nectarines, stoned and cut into chunky slices
50g/2oz demerara sugar
whipped cream or crème fraîche, to serve

Takes 1–1½ hours • Serves 6

1 Preheat the oven to 220°C/Gas 7/fan oven 200°C. Roll out the pastry and cut out a 28cm/11in circle, using a large dinner plate as a guide. Lift the pastry on to a baking tray with a rim, and twist the pastry edge over itself all the way round the circle to make a rope-like edge. Press down lightly to seal. Chill or freeze for at least 15 minutes.

2 Place a largish frying pan over a medium heat and melt the butter with the lemon juice and toffees. When bubbly, briefly toss in the nectarines, then remove the pan from the heat. Spoon the nectarines over the pastry, pouring over any sauce from the pan.

3 Sprinkle the tart with the demerara sugar and bake for 20–25 minutes until golden, puffed up and caramelised. Leave to cool slightly. Serve with cream or crème fraîche.

• Per serving 408 kcalories, protein 5g, carbohydrate 46g, fat 24g, saturated fat 6g, fibre 1g, added sugar 12g, salt 0.76g

This updated version of the original apple recipe couldn't be simpler – it uses ready-rolled pastry so you don't even need a rolling pin.

Tarte Tatin with Brandy Cream

50g/2oz butter
50g/2oz golden caster sugar
½ tsp ground cinnamon
6 medium Cox's or Egremont Russet
apples, peeled, quartered
and cored
375g pack fresh ready-rolled puff
pastry

FOR THE BRANDY CREAM
200ml carton crème fraîche
2 tbsp icing sugar
1 tbsp brandy or calvados

Takes 50 minutes • Serves 4

1 Preheat the oven to 220°C/Gas 7/fan oven 200°C. Melt the butter in a 20cm/8in tarte tatin tin over a medium heat on the hob. Stir in the sugar and heat until starting to caramelise. Stir in the cinnamon. Pile in the apples and cook over a medium heat for about 10 minutes, stirring occasionally, until thickened and saucy. Remove from the heat.
2 Unroll the pastry. Prick it all over with a fork. Lay the pastry over the apples. Trim off any excess, leaving a 2cm/¾in rim. Tuck the pastry round the apples, down the inside of the tin. Bake for 20–30 minutes until risen and golden.
3 Mix the ingredients for the brandy cream. When the tart is cooked, leave in the tin for 5 minutes, then run the blade of a knife round the edge. Invert a plate on top and turn out the tart and juices. Serve with the brandy cream.

• Per serving 761 kcalories, protein 8g, carbohydrate 77g, fat 48g, saturated fat 15g, fibre 3g, added sugar 21g, salt 1.12g

Try finely grated orange zest in the pastry instead of cinnamon.

Rhubarb, Soured Cream and Cinnamon Tart

175g/6oz plain flour
1 tsp ground cinnamon
25g/1oz icing sugar
85g/3oz unsalted butter, chilled and diced
1 egg yolk

FOR THE FILLING
350g/12oz prepared rhubarb, cut into 4cm/1½in lengths
85g/3oz demerara or light muscovado sugar
284ml carton soured cream
25g/1oz caster sugar, plus 1 tsp
1 egg
½ tsp ground cinnamon

Takes 1 hour 20 minutes, plus chilling • Serves 4–6

1 Sift the flour, cinnamon, icing sugar and a pinch of salt into a processor. Add the butter and process to crumbs. Add the egg yolk and 2 tablespoons cold water. Process until it forms a ball. Wrap in foil and chill for 45 minutes.
2 Preheat the oven to 200°C/Gas 6/fan oven 180°C. Roll out pastry to line a 23cm/9in loose-bottomed tin, 4cm/1½in deep. Fork the base. Line with foil. Bake for 10–15 minutes to a pale colour. Remove the foil, scatter in the rhubarb, then the sugar, and bake for 20 minutes.
3 Remove from the oven and reduce the heat to 160°C/Gas 3/fan oven 140°C. Beat the soured cream, 25g/1oz caster sugar and the egg. Pour over the rhubarb. Mix the remaining caster sugar with the cinnamon. Scatter over the tart. Return to the oven for 10–15 minutes or until just set. Cool before serving.

• Per serving for four 642 kcalories, protein 10g, carbohydrate 75g, fat 35g, saturated fat 21g, fibre 3g, added sugar 37g, salt 0.15g

A sensational tart, with a pâtisserie-style finish,
that's surprisingly easy to make.

Greengage and Custard Tart

250g/9oz ready-made shortcrust
pastry
900g/2lb greengages, halved and
stoned
50g/2oz golden caster sugar
1 egg, beaten, for glazing
5 tbsp bought custard, plus extra
to serve
icing sugar, for sprinkling

Takes 1 hour • Serves 6

1 Preheat the oven to 220°C/Gas 7/fan oven 200°C and put a baking sheet in to heat. Meanwhile, roll out the pastry to a 30cm/12in diameter round. Put it on a baking sheet (not the one in the oven). Pile the fruit into the centre, leaving a 2.5cm/1in edge. Sprinkle with all but 1 tablespoon of the sugar. Fold in the pastry edges, and pinch around the fruit.
2 Brush the pastry with beaten egg and sprinkle with the remaining sugar. Using a fish slice, slide it onto the hot baking sheet. Bake for 30 minutes until the pastry is golden and the greengages are tender. Towards the end of cooking, preheat the grill to high.
3 Remove the tart from the oven. Drizzle with the custard. Grill for 2–3 minutes until the edges of the fruit caramelise. Sift icing sugar over and serve warm, with extra custard.

• Per serving 315 kcalories, protein 5g, carbohydrate 44g, fat 14g, saturated fat 6g, fibre 4g, added sugar 11g, salt 0.23g

Don't be put off by the long method and cooking time –
you'll adore the sensational flavours.

Apricot Crème Brûlée Tart

140g/5oz butter
100g/4oz golden caster sugar
250g/9oz plain flour
25g/1oz ground almonds
1 egg, beaten

FOR THE FILLING
250g pack ready-to-eat dried
apricots
175ml/6fl oz sweet dessert wine
such as Sauternes
100g/4oz golden caster sugar, plus
4 tbsp to brûlée
284ml carton double cream
1 vanilla pod, split and seeds
scraped
4 eggs, whisked

Takes a staggered 3 hours •
Serves 10

1 Beat the butter and sugar until pale. Mix in the flour, almonds and egg to make a dough. Wrap and chill for 30 minutes. Put the apricots in a bowl. Bring the wine and sugar to a boil, pour over the apricots and set aside. Bring the cream and vanilla to a boil. Remove from the heat and leave to infuse. Preheat oven to 220°C/Gas 7/fan oven 200°C.
2 Roll the pastry into a 23cm/9in fluted tart tin. Freeze for 10 minutes. Cook for 20 minutes with foil and beans, 5 minutes without. Remove. Reduce oven to 160°C/Gas 3/fan oven 140°C.
3 Strain the vanilla mix over the eggs. Whisk. Drain the apricots. Stir the liquid into the eggs. Pull the apricots apart. Put the sticky sides down on the pastry. Pour the eggs over. Bake for 30 minutes until set. Cool. Scatter the rest of the sugar over. Caramelise with a blowtorch.

• Per serving 510 kcalories, protein 8g, carbohydrate 52g, fat 30g, saturated fat 17g, fibre 3g, added sugar 20g, salt 0.42g

This has got to be the simplest summer tart ever –
a must for anyone who loves blueberries.

Cinnamon Blueberry Tart

2 tsp ground cinnamon
6 tbsp golden caster sugar
375g pack ready-made shortcrust
pastry
200g tub soft cheese
finely grated zest and juice 1 orange
2 tbsp icing sugar, plus extra for
dusting
2 × 150g punnets blueberries

Takes 30 minutes • Serves 6–8

1 Preheat the oven to 200°C/Gas 6/fan oven 180°C. Line a baking sheet with baking parchment. Mix the cinnamon and caster sugar. Scatter the cinnamon sugar over the work surface, then roll out the pastry on top of the sugar, to the thickness of 2 × £1 coins. Using a large dinner plate, cut out a round, about 23cm/9in, and lift onto the baking sheet. Prick the pastry all over with a fork and crimp round the edge with finger and thumb. Chill for 15 minutes.
2 Bake the pastry for 10–12 minutes until dry and biscuity. Cool, then transfer to a plate.
3 Beat the soft cheese with the orange juice and zest. Add icing sugar to taste. Spread this over the pastry base, leaving a 2.5cm/1in border around the edge. Top with the blueberries and dust with icing sugar. Serve.

• Per serving for six 487 kcalories, protein 6g, carbohydrate 56g, fat 28g, saturated fat 15g, fibre 2.1g, added sugar 22.7g, salt 0.54g

Prepare this dessert up to a day ahead to save yourself time.
It's lovely to make and even better to eat.

Chocolate Tart with Raspberries

FOR THE PASTRY
100g/4oz plain flour
50g/2oz ground almonds
85g/3oz butter, cut into small pieces
25g/1oz golden caster sugar
1 egg yolk

FOR THE FILLING
150g bar dark chocolate, in pieces
2 egg whites
100g/4oz golden caster sugar
142ml carton double cream
2 tbsp brandy or Tia Maria

TO SERVE
284ml carton double cream, whipped
300g/10oz raspberries
125g punnet blueberries
icing sugar, for dusting

Takes 1½ hours, plus chilling •
Serves 6–8

1 Put the flour, almonds and butter in a processor and process into crumbs. Add the sugar, egg yolk and 1 tablespoon cold water. Wrap in cling film. Chill for 15–20 minutes.
2 Preheat the oven to 190°C/Gas 5/fan oven 170°C. Roll out the dough and use to line a 24cm/9½in flan tin. Bake blind (with foil and beans) for 15 minutes, then remove the foil and beans and cook for 7–10 minutes more until crisp and golden. Cool.
3 For the filling, melt the chocolate. Put the egg whites and sugar in a bowl over a pan of simmering water. Whisk for 5 minutes until thick and glossy. Remove from the heat and whisk for 2 more minutes. Fold in the chocolate, cream and brandy. Pour into the pastry case. Chill until set, then serve with the whipped cream, berries and icing sugar.

• Per serving for six 794 kcalories, protein 8g, carbohydrate 59g, fat 59g, saturated fat 34g, fibre 3g, added sugar 39g, salt 0.42g

It's so easy to make this deconstructed strawberry tart. If you can't get strawberries, try other summer berries, or sliced peaches or nectarines.

Strawberry Toffee Tart

175g/6oz crunchy biscuits, such as Hobnobs
85g/3oz butter, melted
400g/14oz strawberries
284ml tub double cream
5 soft toffees (such as Werther's Original)
200g tub Greek yogurt
icing sugar, for dusting

Takes 45 minutes • Serves 6

1 Line a 20cm/8in flan tin with baking parchment. Put the biscuits in a strong food bag and bash with a rolling pin to crush them finely. Tip into a bowl and mix in the melted butter. Press over the base of the tin. Chill for about 30 minutes until it feels firm. Slice or halve the strawberries, depending on their size.

2 Remove the biscuit base from the flan tin and slide it onto a flat serving plate. Put 2 tablespoons of the cream in a small bowl with the toffees. Whip the rest until it just holds its shape in soft folds. Fold in the yogurt, then spoon over the biscuit base and cover with the strawberries.

3 Melt the toffees and cream in the microwave on Medium for 30 seconds–1 minute, then stir until they form a sauce. Drizzle over the tart filling. Dust with icing sugar before serving.

• Per serving 559 kcalories, protein 6g, carbohydrate 32g, fat 46g, saturated fat 24g, fibre 2g, added sugar 12g, salt 0.75g

You do need to stone the apricots here, but after that everything is easy.
The icing sugar caramelises deliciously over the fruit.

Apricot and Almond Bistro Tart

370g pack ready-rolled puff pastry
50g/2oz ground almonds
900g/2lb ripe fresh apricots, halved
and stoned
2 tbsp icing sugar
maple syrup and clotted or single
cream, to serve (optional)

Takes 30–40 minutes • Serves 8

1 Preheat the oven to 220°C/Gas 7/fan oven 200°C. Unroll the pastry on to a lightly dampened baking sheet (this creates steam, which helps puff up the pastry), then sprinkle over the ground almonds. Lay the apricot halves over the top, nestling them closely together, right up to the edge of the pastry.
2 Dust with the icing sugar and bake for 20–25 minutes until the sugar starts to caramelise a little.
3 If you like, drizzle with maple syrup and serve hot, warm or cold. If you really want to indulge, serve with a spoonful of clotted cream or a pouring of single cream.

• Per serving 258 kcalories, protein 5g, carbohydrate 29g, fat 14g, saturated fat none, fibre 2g, added sugar 4g, salt 0.37g

Don't be put off by the idea of goat's cheese in a dessert – when soft and fresh it works beautifully, like a richly flavoured crème fraîche.

Sweet Lemon and Goat's Cheese Tart

500g pack ready-made sweet shortcrust pastry
4 eggs, beaten
zest and juice of 2 lemons
140g/5oz caster sugar
200ml carton crème fraîche
100g pack rindless fresh goat's cheese, roughly crumbled
blackberries or other fruit, to serve

Takes 1 hours 40 minutes, plus chilling • Serves 6

1 Preheat the oven to 180°C/Gas 4/fan oven 160°C. Roll out the pastry and use to line a 20cm/8in loose-bottomed tart tin, about 3–4 cm/1¼–1½ in deep. Chill for 30 minutes.
2 Line the pastry with foil and beans. Bake for 15 minutes. Remove the foil and beans, brush the inside of the tart with a little beaten egg, then return to the oven for 5 minutes to crisp. Remove from the oven. Reduce the heat to 150°C/Gas 2/fan oven 130°C.
3 Mix the lemon zest, juice and sugar until the sugar dissolves, then beat in the remaining eggs and crème fraîche. Tip into a jug. Put the tart case on a baking sheet in the oven and pour in the lemon mixture. Sprinkle over the goat's cheese. Bake for 1 hour–1 hour 10 minutes, until set with a slight wobble. Serve warm or cold, with fruit.

• Per serving 710 kcalories, protein 12g, carbohydrate 66g, fat 46g, saturated fat 20g, fibre 2g, added sugar 33g, salt 0.79g

For this new take on a classic, the pavlova is filled with spoonfuls of semi-freddo (half-frozen soft-scoop ice cream) instead of cream.

Raspberry Ripple Pavlova

250g/9oz raspberries
50g/2oz icing sugar
250g carton mascarpone
284ml carton double cream, whipped
175g/6oz caster sugar
3 large egg whites, at room temperature, whisked to stiff peaks
1 tsp cornflour
handful unsalted pistachios, sliced

Takes 2 hours, plus freezing • Serves 6

1 Sieve 140g/5oz of the raspberries, leaving behind the seeds. Stir in half the icing sugar. Whisk the mascarpone into the cream until thick. Stir in the remaining icing sugar. Drop spoonfuls into a deep plastic container. Drizzle some sieved raspberries over. Don't stir. Add another layer of cream and raspberries. Smooth the top. Freeze for 2–2½ hours until half frozen.
2 Preheat the oven to 140°C/Gas 1/fan oven 120°C. Line a baking sheet with non-stick parchment. Draw a 20–23cm/8–9in circle on the paper. Slowly whisk the caster sugar into the egg whites until thick. Beat in the cornflour. Pile the meringue onto the paper circle. Scatter over the pistachios. Bake for 1¼–1½ hours until crisp outside. Cool, then peel off the paper.
3 Pile spoonfuls of semi-freddo on the pavlova. Scatter over the remaining raspberries. Serve.

• Per serving 593 kcalories, protein 5g, carbohydrate 46g, fat 44g, saturated fat 27g, fibre 1g, added sugar 38g, salt 0.59g

Make the most of home-grown rhubarb
with this impressive dessert.

Rhubarb and Ginger Pavlova

2 tsp cornflour
1 tsp white vinegar
1 tsp vanilla extract
5 egg whites
300g/10oz caster sugar

FOR THE TOPPING
450g/1lb prepared rhubarb, cut into
2.5cm/1in lengths
2 pieces preserved stem ginger in
syrup, finely chopped, plus 2 tbsp
of the syrup
100g/4oz caster sugar
finely grated zest of 1 lime
425ml/¾ pint double cream, softly
whipped

Takes 2½ hours, plus cooling
• Serves 8

1 Preheat the oven to 140°C/Gas 1/fan oven 120°C. Line a baking sheet with non-stick parchment. Draw a 23cm/9in circle on it. Mix the cornflour, vinegar and vanilla. Whisk the egg whites until stiff. Slowly whisk in the cornflour mixture and sugar until stiff. Spoon onto the circle. Make a slight dip in the centre. Bake for 1 hour. Turn off the oven and leave the pavlova in. When cold, remove the paper.
2 Turn up the oven to 190°C/Gas 5/fan oven 170°C. Put the rhubarb, ginger syrup, sugar and 2 tablespoons water in an ovenproof dish. Bake for 15 minutes until the rhubarb is tender. Cool. Drain the juices into a pan. Fast boil for 5 minutes until syrupy.
3 Fold the ginger and lime zest into the cream. Pile onto the pavlova. Top with rhubarb. Spoon over some syrup; serve the rest separately.

• Per serving 468 kcalories, protein 3g, carbohydrate 60g, fat 26g, saturated fat 16g, fibre 1g, added sugar 56g, salt 0.2g

Pavlovas are always popular. This is the one to try if you're looking for a fresh idea – it's simply bursting with Mediterranean flavours.

Apricot and Pistachio Pavlova

2 tsp cornflour
2 tsp vanilla extract
2 tsp white wine or cider vinegar
5 large egg whites, whisked until stiff
300g/10oz golden caster sugar
50g/2oz shelled pistachio nuts, roughly chopped
650g/1lb 7oz ripe fresh apricots
3 tbsp Cointreau or other orange-flavoured liqueur
4 tbsp icing sugar, or more to taste
568ml carton double cream, lightly whipped

Takes 1¾–2 hours, plus cooling • Serves 6

1 Preheat the oven to 140°C/Gas 1/fan oven 120°C. Line a baking sheet with non-stick parchment. Mix the cornflour, vanilla extract and vinegar. Slowly whisk in the sugar with the eggs until thick. Whisk in the cornflour paste.
2 Spoon the mixture on to the paper. Spread to a 23cm/9in round. Swirl the edges. Scatter half the pistachios over and bake for 1 hour, until crisp. Turn off the oven and leave the pavlova to cool with the oven door open.
3 Reserve 450g/1lb of the apricots. Roughly chop the rest, purée them, then push them through a sieve. Stir in the liqueur and add icing sugar to taste. Spoon the cream over the pavlova. Slice the reserved apricots. Scatter them over the cream with the remaining pistachios. Dust with icing sugar and serve with the apricot purée.

• Per serving 789 kcalories, protein 7g, carbohydrate 78g, fat 50g, saturated fat 29g, fibre 2g, added sugar 65g, salt 0.26g

An unusual pudding where the sponge and meringue bake together.

Strawberries and Cream Meringue Cake

FOR THE CAKE
100g/4oz butter, at room temperature, plus extra for greasing
100g/4oz golden caster sugar
1 large egg, plus 2 egg yolks (keep the whites for the meringue)
85g/3oz self-raising flour
25g/1oz shelled pistachios, finely ground
2 tbsp milk

FOR THE MERINGUE
2 large egg whites
100g/4oz golden caster sugar

FOR THE TOPPING
284ml carton double cream, softly whipped
200g/8oz strawberries, hulled, sliced or left whole

Takes 1¼ hours • Serves 8

1 Preheat the oven to 180°C/Gas 4/fan oven 160°C. For the cake, butter and line the bottom of a 20cm/8in round, loose-bottomed sandwich tin with greaseproof paper. Beat the butter and sugar together for 3–4 minutes until pale and creamy. Beat in the egg and egg yolks. Gently stir in the flour and ground nuts alternately with the milk. Spoon into the tin and level it smooth.
2 Make the meringue. Whisk the egg whites until stiff. Whisk in the sugar, a couple of spoonfuls at a time, until smooth and glossy. Spoon into the tin and spread it. Bake for 45 minutes until the meringue feels crisp.
3 Leave in the tin to cool, then loosen the edges with a knife and remove. Peel off the paper and leave until cold. Spoon the cream over the meringue, then the strawberries.

• Per serving 446 kcalories, protein 5g, carbohydrate 37g, fat 32g, saturated fat 18g, fibre 1g, added sugar 26g, salt 0.46g

A gorgeous summer dessert, using the best
of the season's fruit.

Baby Pavlovas with Summer Fruits

85g/3oz shelled pistachios, or
hazelnuts
1 tsp cornflour
1 tsp white wine vinegar
200g/8oz golden caster sugar
4 egg whites, whisked to soft peaks

FOR THE FILLING
200ml carton crème fraîche
450g/1lb seasonal berries, such as
strawberries, raspberries,
blueberries, redcurrants, or
blackberries

Takes 1¼–1½ hours • Serves 4

1 Preheat the oven to 140°C/Gas 1/fan oven 120°C. Line a baking sheet with non-stick parchment. Toast the nuts in a shallow roasting tin in the oven for 7–10 minutes until golden. Coarsely grind in a processor. Blend the cornflour and vinegar. Slowly add the sugar to the eggs a tablespoon at a time until you get a stiff, glossy mixture.
2 Reserve 2 tablespoons of the nuts and fold the rest into the meringue, then stir in the cornflour mixture. Spoon the mixture on to the baking sheet to make four pavlovas. Hollow out a dip in the centres. Sprinkle with the reserved nuts and bake for 45 minutes until crisp on the outside. Turn off the oven, but leave the meringues until completely cold.
3 Spoon a little crème fraîche into the middle of each pavlova. Scatter over the fruit to serve.

• Per serving 552 kcalories, protein 9g, carbohydrate 61g, fat 32g, saturated fat 14g, fibre 2g, added sugar 53g, salt 0.23g

These dinky pavlovas are sure to prove a family favourite, perfect for special occasions.

Pear and Chocolate Pavlovas

FOR THE MERINGUES
2 medium egg whites
175g/6oz caster sugar
1 tsp cornflour
½ tsp white wine vinegar

FOR THE PEARS
8 small pears, peeled
2 tbsp runny honey
300ml/½ pint apple juice
1 cinnamon stick

FOR THE CHOCOLATE SAUCE
142ml carton double cream
100g bar dark chocolate, broken into pieces

FOR THE FILLING
284ml carton whipping cream
200g/8oz half-fat Greek yogurt

Takes 1½ hours • Serves 8

1 Preheat the oven to 140°C/Gas 1/fan oven 120°C. Line two large baking sheets with parchment. Whisk the egg whites until stiff. Slowly whisk in the sugar until stiff. Beat in the cornflour and the vinegar. Spoon 8 mounds on the parchment. Spread each to a 9cm/3½in circle, with a dip in the centres. Bake for 40–50 minutes until crisp. Remove the paper. Cool.
2 With a sharp knife, scoop out the cores from underneath the pears, leaving the stalks on. Fit the pears in a pan. Add the honey, apple juice and cinnamon. Bring to the boil, lower the heat, cover and simmer for 35–40 minutes until tender. Remove the lid, raise the heat and bubble briefly to a glaze. Cool the pears in it.
3 Melt the chocolate and cream. For the filling, stir the cream and yogurt until thick. Top the meringues with the filling, pears and sauce.

• Per serving 441 kcalories, protein 4.9g, carbohydrate 43g, fat 28.9g, saturated fat 17.5g, fibre 1.8g, added sugar 28.2g, salt 0.18g

Homemade blackcurrant sorbet is a revelation – bursting with flavours it freezes to a beautiful, rich burgundy colour.

Blackcurrant and Mint Sorbet

200g/8oz golden caster sugar
20g pack fresh mint, plus some small sprigs to serve
750g/1lb 10oz blackcurrants
4 tbsp liquid glucose
juice of 2 lemons

Takes 30–35 minutes, plus freezing • Serves 4–6

1 Make a syrup by stirring the sugar with 200ml/7fl oz boiling water until dissolved, then steep the mint in it until cool – about 15 minutes. Discard the mint.

2 Cook the blackcurrants in the syrup with the glucose for about 5 minutes until the fruit is soft. Whizz in a food processor, then strain into a bowl through a sieve (not nylon), rubbing with the back of a ladle or spoon to remove the pips. Stir in the lemon juice and cool.

3 Freeze in an ice cream machine according to the manufacturer's instructions until it becomes a thick slush, then scoop into a freezer container and freeze. Alternatively pour into a shallow freezer container and beat three or four times as it freezes. Before serving, allow to thaw and soften for about 10 minutes, then serve with sprigs of fresh mint.

• Per serving for four 301 kcalories, protein 2g, carbohydrate 78g, fat none, saturated fat none, fibre 7g, added sugar 56g, salt 0.08g

Serve individual portions in
shot or cocktail glasses.

Redcurrant Sorbet

450g/1lb redcurrants, plus extra
for decoration
2 tbsp elderflower cordial
140g/5oz golden caster sugar

Takes 40 minutes • Serves 4

1 Remove the redcurrants from their stems,
wash them and put them in a pan with
2 tablespoons water. Bring to the boil, lower
the heat, cover and simmer for 5 minutes
until softened. Push through a sieve to make
a purée. Stir in the elderflower cordial and
set to one side to cool.
2 Put the caster sugar in a pan with
300ml/½ pint water and stir over a low heat
for 5 minutes until the sugar has dissolved.
Raise the heat and boil for 10 minutes.
3 Tip the redcurrant mixture into the syrup
and mix. Return to the boil, turn the heat down
and simmer for 2 minutes. Cool, pour into a
freezer container and freeze for 3–4 hours
until frozen. Scoop into small glasses and
serve topped with redcurrants.

• Per serving 178 kcalories, protein 1g, carbohydrate
46g, fat none, saturated fat none, fibre 4g, added
sugar 41g, salt 0.01g

For caffeine addicts everywhere,
this is the perfect treat for one.

Iced Coffee Sundae

1 shot of cold espresso coffee or 30ml/1fl oz strong black coffee
200ml/7fl oz full-fat milk
3 scoops vanilla ice cream
2 ice cubes
1 small brownie or chocolate chip cookie

Takes 5 minutes • Serves 1

1 Pour the espresso or strong coffee and milk into a blender.
2 Add 2 scoops of ice cream and the ice cubes, then blitz until it is the consistency of a smoothie.
3 Pour straight into a tall glass, top with the last scoop of ice cream and crumble over the brownie or cookie to finish.

• Per serving 575 kcalories, protein 14g, carbohydrate 66g, fat 30g, saturated fat 19g, fibre 1g, added sugar 36g, salt 0.70g

You don't have to use vanilla ice cream –
try using scoops of your favourite flavour.

Melba Sundaes

150g punnet raspberries
1–2 tsp icing sugar, to sweeten
1 peach
4–6 scoops of vanilla ice cream

Takes 10 minutes • Serves 2

1 Blitz half the raspberries in a blender with enough icing sugar to sweeten (or mash well with a fork). Set aside.

2 Halve, stone and thinly slice a peach. Divide it between two tall glasses, layering it with the remaining whole berries and scoops of ice cream.

3 Finish off with a drizzle of the raspberry sauce.

• Per serving 260 kcalories, protein 6g, carbohydrate 34g, fat 12g, saturated fat 7.8g, fibre 2.7g, added sugar 22.2g, salt 0.19g

You can store this ice cream for up to 1 month in the freezer.

Blueberry, Coconut and Lime Ice Cream

2 limes
140g/5oz golden caster sugar
125g punnet blueberries
200ml carton coconut cream
284ml carton double cream
extra blueberries and lime wedges, to serve

Takes 20–25 minutes, plus freezing • Serves 4–6

1 Finely grate the zest from one of the limes. Squeeze the juice from both. Put in a small pan with the sugar. Heat gently, stirring to dissolve the sugar. Add the blueberries and simmer for 2 minutes, until the skins start to split.
2 Pour the blueberry mixture into a bowl. Stir in the coconut cream. Cool. Whip the cream until it just holds its shape, then gradually stir in the blueberry mixture. Put the bowl in the freezer for about 1 hour, until the mixture is set about 3cm/1¼in in from the edges.
3 Remove from the freezer and whisk it all together. When it's fairly smooth, return to the freezer for 1 hour. Repeat the whisking. Transfer the ice cream to a rigid container, cover and freeze until firm. Before serving, move to the fridge for 30 minutes to soften. Serve with extra blueberries and lime wedges.

• Per serving for six 429 kcalories, protein 3g, carbohydrate 29g, fat 35g, saturated fat 24g, fibre 1g, added sugar 25g, salt 0.05g

A delicious semi-frozen parfait flavoured with lemon curd,
ripe summer strawberries and crunchy meringue.

Eton Mess Parfait

284ml carton double cream
200ml tub Greek yogurt
4 small meringues, crumbled
(shop-bought is fine)
200g/8oz strawberries, hulled and
chopped
2 tbsp lemon curd
strawberries, halved, and
raspberries, to serve

FOR THE BERRY SAUCE
150g punnet raspberries
150g punnet strawberries
2 tbsp icing sugar
1 tbsp lemon juice

Takes 15 minutes, plus freezing •
Serves 6

1 Line 6 × 150ml/¼ pint ramekin dishes with cling film. Lightly whip the cream, then fold in the yogurt, meringues and strawberries until well combined. Fold in the lemon curd to give a soft marbled effect. Spoon into the prepared ramekins and freeze for 2–2½ hours or until semi-frozen.

2 Meanwhile, make the berry sauce. Tip the raspberries, strawberries, icing sugar and lemon juice into a food processor and blend to a purée. Pass the sauce through a sieve to remove the pips, then set aside.

3 To serve, turn the semi-frozen parfaits out onto serving plates and remove the cling film. Arrange halved strawberries and raspberries on top of the parfaits. Serve with a drizzle of berry sauce.

• Per serving 576 kcalories, protein 7g, carbohydrate 43g, fat 43g, saturated fat 24g, fibre 3g, added sugar 28g, salt 0.21g

This recipe is not only easy to make, but looks and tastes so good it's hard to believe it only takes 20 minutes to put together.

Lemon Meringue Ice Cream

bought slab Madeira cake
8 meringue nests
500ml tub crème fraîche
jar good quality lemon curd
red summer berries, to decorate

Takes 25 minutes, plus freezing •
Serves 8

1 Line the base of a 20cm/8in round spring-form cake tin with greaseproof paper. Cut the Madeira cake into 1cm/½in slices and use to line the base of the tin. Fill in the gaps between the slices with small pieces of cake.
2 Break the meringues into pieces and put into a large bowl. Fold in the crème fraîche. Dollop large spoonfuls of the meringue mixture and lemon curd into the tin. Don't stir. Level with a palette knife, then tap the tin to pack down the mixture. Freeze for at least 4 hours.
3 When ready to serve, remove the cake from the tin and put on a serving plate. (If made a day or more ahead, put in the fridge for 20 minutes before serving.) Decorate with red summer berries and serve.

• Per serving 464 kcalories, protein 5g, carbohydrate 57g, fat 26g, saturated fat 14g, fibre 1g, added sugar 37g, salt 0.51g

Homemade ice cream looks so impressive and
this one is deliciously different.

Pecan Banana Ice Cream

5 ripe bananas
225ml/8fl oz orange juice, fresh or
from a carton
568ml carton double cream
225g/8oz golden caster sugar
100g/4oz pecan halves

FOR THE BOURBON SAUCE
85g/3oz light muscovado sugar
1 tbsp cornflour
50g/2oz butter
6 tbsp bourbon

Takes 20 minutes • Serves 6

1 Mash the bananas in a large bowl. Beat in the orange juice, cream and 175g/6oz of the sugar. Slowly heat the remaining sugar in a small heavy-based pan with 2 tablespoons cold water to dissolve the sugar. Boil hard, without stirring, to a light caramel colour. Remove from the heat and stir in the pecans.
2 Tip onto an oiled sheet of foil. Cool. Roughly chop and stir into the banana mix. Pour into a large rigid plastic container and freeze for at least 4 hours, or overnight. Transfer to the fridge 30 minutes before serving.
3 For the sauce, mix the sugar and cornflour in a small pan. Gradually stir in 300ml/½ pint boiling water. Bring slowly to the boil, stirring until smooth. Add the butter and bourbon. Stir until melted. Pour over the ice cream and serve.

• Per serving 941 kcalories, protein 4g, carbohydrate 83g, fat 64g, saturated fat 33g, fibre 2g, added sugar 54g, salt 0.28g

In just 20 minutes you can make
the perfect summer dessert.

Summer Ice Cream Trifles

500g/1lb 2oz strawberries, hulled
3 tbsp golden caster sugar
8 thin slices bought Madeira cake
(just over ½ × 225g cake)
2 tbsp strawberry jam
juice of 1 large orange
500g tub chilled custard
4–6 generous scoops vanilla ice
cream

Takes 20 minutes, plus chilling •
Makes 4 large or 6 small

1 Tip the strawberries into a food processor, sprinkle over the sugar and whizz together until the strawberries are completely puréed.
2 Spread four slices of cake with jam and sandwich them in pairs with the remaining slices. Cut each sandwich into small cubes, divide among four large or six small glasses, then drizzle over the orange juice.
3 Pour the custard over the cake and spoon the strawberry purée on top. Chill the trifles until you are ready to eat. (They can be made up to this stage 1 day ahead.) Top with scoops of vanilla ice cream just before serving.

• Per small trifle 586 kcalories, protein 11g, carbohydrate 94g, fat 21g, saturated fat 12g, fibre 2g, added sugar 54g, salt 0.93g

As there's no cream in this luscious pudding, it's delightfully light.

Cheesecake Bombe with Summer Fruits

2 × 250g cartons curd or ricotta cheese
100g/4oz icing sugar
finely grated zest of 1 large orange
500g tub low-fat fromage frais
600g/1lb 5oz strawberries
250g/9oz raspberries
150g punnet blueberries or *fraises des bois* (wild strawberries)
icing sugar, for dusting

FOR THE SAUCE
350g/12oz mixed summer fruits, such as strawberries (hulled), raspberries and blueberries (fresh or frozen)
juice of 1 large orange
4 tbsp icing sugar
3 tbsp crème de cassis or crème de mûre (blackberry liqueur), optional

Takes 30 minutes, plus several hours draining • Serves 6–8

1 Beat together the cheese, sugar and zest. Fold in the fromage frais. Line a large sieve, colander or two new traditionally shaped terracotta flowerpots (10–12cm/4–4½in across the top) with muslin or a clean J-cloth and spoon in the mixture, pressing it down firmly. Set over a bowl and put in the fridge for at least 4 hours or overnight to drain off the liquid and firm up the mixture.

2 Tip all the sauce ingredients into a food processor and blitz until smooth, then press through a sieve.

3 Hull the strawberries and halve if large. Mix with the other fruits.

4 Turn the cheesecake out on to one large or two smaller platters and remove the cloth. Surround with the fruit and dust with icing sugar. Serve the sauce in a serving jug.

• Per serving for six 358 kcalories, protein 21g, carbohydrate 49g, fat 10g, saturated fat 6g, fibre 4g, added sugar 27g, salt 1.06g

This is a wonderful fuss-free dinner-party dessert
that can be made several hours in advance.

Strawberry Cheesecake Crunchies

40g/1½oz butter
125ml/4fl oz double cream
100g/4oz golden caster sugar
25g/1oz flaked almonds
25g/1oz shelled pistachios, chopped
50g/2oz plain flour

FOR THE FILLING AND
DECORATION
200g packet full-fat soft cheese
397g can sweetened condensed milk
finely grated zest of 2 lemons and
8 tbsp juice
142ml carton double cream,
lightly whipped
450g/1lb strawberries, hulled
2 tbsp golden caster sugar
2 tbsp redcurrant jelly

Takes 40–45 minute, plus chilling •
Serves 6

1 Preheat the oven to 180°C/Gas 4/fan oven 160°C. Line a baking sheet with non-stick parchment. Slowly bring the butter, cream and sugar to the boil, stirring. Take off the heat. Stir in the nuts and flour. Spread half the mixture in a 20cm/8in round on the sheet. Bake for 10–12 minutes until golden. Cool briefly on the sheet, then put on a rack to firm. Repeat.
2 Beat the cheese. Slowly beat in the milk, lemon and whipped cream. Chill for 2–4 hours until softly set. Sieve 4 strawberries into a pan. Add the sugar and jelly. Heat gently, stirring to dissolve. Boil for 2–3 minutes until syrupy. Cool.
3 Slice the remaining strawberries. Break the biscuit into shards. Layer the cheese mixture, strawberries, syrup and biscuit in glasses, saving a few pieces. Chill for 2 hours. Top with the remaining biscuit.

• Per serving 698 kcalories, protein 14g, carbohydrate 84g, fat 37g, saturated fat 17g, fibre 1g, added sugar 59g, salt 0.44g

If either of the juices do set when you don't want them to,
simply sit them in a bowl of very hot water to redissolve.

Cranberry Sunrise

10 gelatine leaves
700ml/1¼ pints smooth-style orange juice
700ml/1¼ pints cranberry juice

Takes 10–15 minutes, plus setting • Serves 8–10

1 Soak 5 of the gelatine leaves in a little cold water in a bowl for 5 minutes to soften. Drain, squeeze the soaked gelatine and return to the bowl. Pour over 100ml/3½fl oz hot (not boiling) water from the kettle and stir to dissolve.
2 Warm the orange juice in a pan and stir in the dissolved gelatine. Set aside. Dissolve the rest of the gelatine leaves in the same way as above. Warm the cranberry juice in a pan and pour in the dissolved gelatine. Pour half the orange mixture into a 2½ pint/ 1.4 litre jelly mould. Chill until completely set – about 4 hours. (Keep the other juices at room temperature so they don't set.)
3 Cover the set orange jelly with half the cranberry jelly and chill to set. Repeat the process until both juices are used. Leave to set overnight.

• Per serving for eight 104 kcalories, protein 7g, carbohydrate 20g, fat none, saturated fat none, fibre 0.1g, added sugar 9.3g, salt 0.09g

Sophisticated, simple and foolproof.
Make sure your peaches are really ripe.

Marsala-soused Peaches

500ml/18fl oz Marsala wine
1 vanilla pod, halved lengthways
6 ripe peaches (9 if you want seconds), halved and stoned
227g carton clotted cream
almond biscuits, to serve

Takes 30 minutes, plus chilling • Serves 6

1 Pour the Marsala into a wide shallow pan (large enough to take all the peaches in a single layer) and bring to the boil. Lower the heat, add the vanilla pod and simmer gently for 15 minutes until reduced by nearly two-thirds to about 200ml/7fl oz.

2 Carefully tuck in the peaches and cook gently, uncovered, for about 5 minutes, until starting to soften, turning frequently. Leave to cool in the pan, then tip into a big serving bowl and chill for at least 1 hour, turning occasionally, until you are ready to serve. (You can prepare to this stage up to 8 hours ahead.)

3 To serve, spoon the peaches and juices into bowls and serve with a dollop of clotted cream and the biscuits.

• Per serving 355 kcalories, protein 2g, carbohydrate 14g, fat 24g, saturated fat 15g, fibre 2g, added sugar none, salt 0.08g

White chocolate and coconut milk form the base of this parfait,
which will keep in the freezer for up to a month.

Iced Strawberry Parfait

400ml can coconut milk
200g block white chocolate, broken
into pieces
200g/8oz strawberries, hulled
4 tbsp icing sugar
284ml carton double cream
2 tbsp Malibu

FOR THE SALSA
3 tbsp icing sugar
3 tbsp Malibu
400g/14oz strawberries, hulled and
chopped

Takes 35 minutes, plus freezing •
Serves 8

1 Tip the coconut milk into a small pan and add the chocolate. Warm over a low heat until the chocolate melts, pour into a bowl and cool. Lightly oil the inside of a 1kg/2lb loaf tin and line the base and sides with cling film.
2 Purée 140g/5oz of the strawberries in a processor with 2 tablespoons of the sugar. Rub through a sieve. Thinly slice the remaining strawberries. Whip the cream with the remaining icing sugar and the Malibu until it holds its shape. Fold into the coconut mix with the strawberries and purée. Pour into the tin, then freeze for 5 hours or until firm.
3 Make the salsa. Mix the icing sugar and Malibu with the chopped strawberries and chill. Transfer the parfait to the fridge for 1 hour before serving. Tip out of the tin, strip away the cling film and slice. Serve with the salsa.

• Per serving 406 kcalories, protein 3g, carbohydrate 38g, fat 27g, saturated fat 11g, fibre 1g, added sugar 28g, salt 0.28g

Perfect served with a glass of Asti Spumante
at the end of a summer meal.

Chocolate Berry Cups

284ml carton double cream
100g/4oz dark chocolate, broken
into pieces
1 tbsp icing sugar
550g/1lb 4oz mixed summer fruits
(raspberries, strawberries,
cherries, blueberries), stoned and
halved if necessary

Takes 15 minutes, plus chilling •
Serves 4

1 Heat the cream in a saucepan until just coming to the boil. Remove from the heat, tip in the chocolate pieces, then stir until melted. Cool slightly.

2 Tip the icing sugar and most of the fruit into the pan and mix gently.

3 Spoon into four glasses or cups, top with the remaining fruit, then chill in the fridge until needed (up to 3 hours ahead of serving).

• Per serving 503 kcalories, protein 4g, carbohydrate 31g, fat 41g, saturated fat 25g, fibre 3g, added sugar 20g, salt 0.08g

Lemongrass adds an intriguing citrus taste and fragrance to the syrup for this exotic fruit salad. It's delicious served with mango sorbet.

Tropical Fruits in Lemongrass Syrup

425g can lychees in syrup
2 lemongrass stalks, halved and bashed with a rolling pin
85g/3oz caster sugar
800g/1¾lb mix of prepared tropical fruits, such as papaya, mango, pineapple and melon
100g/4oz seedless red grapes
6 macaroons or coconut biscuits, to serve

Takes 15 minutes, plus chilling • Serves 6

1 Drain the lychees' juice into a pan and put the lychees in a large serving bowl. Add the lemongrass and sugar to the pan.
2 Heat gently until the sugar dissolves, then boil for 1 minute. Turn off the heat and set aside – the lemongrass will add flavour as it cools.
3 Strain the syrup over the lychees and tip in the prepared fruits. Chill. Serve with macaroons or coconut biscuits.

• Per serving 172 kcalories, protein 1g, carbohydrate 44g, fat none, saturated fat none, fibre 3g, added sugar 18g, salt 0.02g

Ideal for entertaining, as they can be kept in the fridge for up to a day.

Coconut Custards with Lime Strawberries

150ml/¼ pint good-quality ready-made custard
100g/4oz creamed coconut in a block
500g/1lb 2oz small strawberries
1 tsp lime juice
85g/3oz icing sugar
250g carton mascarpone
finely grated zest of 2 limes

Takes 30 minutes, plus chilling • Serves 6

1 Pour the custard into a small, heavy-based pan and grate in the creamed coconut. Heat gently until the coconut dissolves, then remove from the heat and leave to cool.

2 Hull and halve two-thirds of the strawberries and put to one side. Blitz the rest with the lime juice and 2 tablespoons of the icing sugar. Set aside. Tip the mascarpone into a large bowl and beat in the cooled coconut custard. Add half of the lime zest and the remaining icing sugar and mix until smooth.

3 Divide the custard mixture between six large glasses. Follow with a layer of strawberry halves. Pour over some strawberry sauce, then finish with another layer of custard. Chill for at least an hour, then top with the remaining lime zest before serving.

• Per serving 406 kcalories, protein 4g, carbohydrate 27g, fat 32g, saturated fat 23g, fibre 3g, added sugar 16g, salt 0.19g

Try this as a chocolatey alternative to Christmas pudding.
It's wonderfully moist, with lashings of chocolate sauce to serve.

Chocolate and Apricot Pud

100g/4oz softened butter, plus extra
200g/8oz ready-to-eat dried apricots
4 tbsp brandy
100g/4oz ground almonds
25g/1oz cocoa powder
100g/4oz self-raising flour
1 tsp baking powder
140g/5oz light muscovado sugar
2 large eggs, beaten
4 tbsp milk
100g/4oz dark chocolate, cut into
large chunks
2 tbsp clear honey

FOR THE SAUCE
100g/4oz dark chocolate, broken
in pieces
284ml carton double cream, plus
extra to serve

Takes 30–40 minutes,
plus 2½ hours steaming • Serves 6–8

1 Butter a 1.2 litre/2 pint pudding basin. Line the base. Put the apricots and brandy in a small pan. Bring slowly to the boil, then simmer. Let the brandy soak in. Cool. Tip the ground almonds into a bowl. Sift over the cocoa, flour and baking powder and stir. In another bowl, beat the butter and sugar until fluffy. Slowly beat in the eggs and milk.
2 Finely chop half the apricots. Fold the flour mix into the cake mix, then the apricots and chocolate. Put the whole apricots into the basin. Spoon over the honey. Add the pudding mixture. Cover tightly and steam for 2½ hours.
3 Near the end of the steaming time, make the sauce. Put the ingredients in a small pan. Warm and stir gently until smooth. Cool the pudding for 10 minutes. Turn out and serve with the chocolate sauce and extra cream.

• Per serving for eight 665 kcalories, protein 9g, carbohydrate 58g, fat 44g, saturated fat 23g, fibre 4g, added sugar 36g, salt 0.74g

A tropical twist on a traditional classic. You can freeze the whole dish in the freezer for up to 1 month. Heat thoroughly before serving.

Mango, Pear and Ginger Crumble

450g/1lb ripe pears peeled, cored and thickly sliced
1 tbsp muscovado sugar
2 mangoes, peeled, stoned and roughly chopped
1 piece stem ginger, finely chopped

FOR THE TOPPING
85g/3oz butter
175g/6oz plain flour
85g/3oz muscovado sugar
85g/3oz pecan nuts, very roughly chopped

Takes 50 minutes • Serves 4

1 Preheat the oven to 180°C/Gas 4/fan oven 160°C. Put the pears in a saucepan with the sugar and 4 tablespoons water. Cook over a gentle heat for 5 minutes until the pears are just tender.

2 Remove from the heat and stir in the mangoes and stem ginger. Spoon the mixture into a not-too-deep 1.7 litre/3 pint baking dish and leave to go cold.

3 Make the topping. Rub the butter into the flour and stir in the sugar and pecan nuts. Sprinkle it all over the fruit and bake for 30 minutes until browned. Serve immediately.

• Per serving 684 kcalories, protein 8g, carbohydrate 95g, fat 33g, saturated fat 11g, fibre 9g, added sugar 26g, salt 0.45g

Light, fluffy and fruity, these pancakes are the
perfect way to celebrate Pancake Day.

American Blueberry Pancakes

200g/8oz self-raising flour
1 tsp baking powder
1 egg
300ml/½ pint milk
knob of butter, melted
150g pack blueberries
sunflower oil or a little butter for
cooking
golden or maple syrup, to serve

Takes 25–35 minutes •
Makes 10 pancakes

1 Mix together the flour, baking powder and a pinch of salt in a large bowl. Beat the egg with the milk, make a well in the centre of the dry ingredients and whisk in the milk to make a thick smooth batter. Beat in the melted butter and gently stir in half the blueberries.
2 Heat a teaspoon of oil or small knob of butter in a large non-stick frying pan. Drop a large tablespoonful of the batter into the pan to make a pancake about 7.5cm/3in across. Make three or four at a time. Cook for about 3 minutes over a medium heat until small bubbles appear on the surface, then turn and cook for another 2–3 minutes, until golden.
3 Cover with kitchen paper to keep warm while you use up the rest of the batter. Serve with golden or maple syrup and the rest of the blueberries.

• Per pancake 108 kcalories, protein 4g, carbohydrate 18g, fat 3g, saturated fat 1g, fibre 1g, added sugar none, salt 0.41g

This bread and butter pudding is irresistible served with a little single cream.

Raisin Bread and Butter Pudding

50g/2oz butter, softened, plus extra
for greasing
400g/14oz raisin loaf, crusts on
750ml/1¼ pints milk
142ml carton double cream
finely grated zest of 1 lemon
4 eggs
50g/2oz golden caster sugar
2 tbsp brandy or 1 tsp vanilla extract

FOR THE TOPPING
2 tbsp demerara sugar
2 tbsp chopped nuts
1 tsp ground cinnamon

Takes 1 hour 20 minutes • Serves 6

1 Butter a shallow ovenproof dish, about 2 litres/3½ pints. Spread each slice of raisin bread with butter (don't use the end crusts). Halve the slices diagonally. Put the milk, cream and lemon zest in a pan. Bring slowly to the boil. Cool to lukewarm.

2 Beat the eggs and sugar. Add the brandy or vanilla and the warm lemon milk. Arrange half the bread over the base of the dish. Pour over half the milk mixture. Repeat the bread and milk layers. Let it soak for 15 minutes. Preheat the oven to 180°C/Gas 4/fan oven 160°C.

3 Mix the topping ingredients. Sprinkle over the pudding. Bake for 40–45 minutes until golden brown and firm. Leave for 5 minutes before serving.

• Per serving 579 kcalories, protein 16g, carbohydrate 57g, fat 32g, saturated fat 15g, fibre none, added sugar 24g, salt 1.03g

This sumptuous American dessert makes a luscious change to crumble.
You can subsitute other fruits if you like – try fruits of the forest.

Apple and Blueberry Cobbler

1 Bramley cooking apple, about
175g/6oz
250g/9oz carton blueberries
50g/2oz light muscovado sugar
250g carton mascarpone

FOR THE COBBLER TOPPING
85g/3oz butter, cut into pieces
225g/8oz self-raising flour
50g/2oz light muscovado sugar
grated zest of 1 lemon
150g carton natural yogurt

Takes 30 minutes • Serves 4

1 Preheat the oven to 220°C/Gas 7/fan oven 200°C. Peel, core and thinly slice the apple and put into a 1.5 litre/2¾ pint ovenproof dish. Scatter over the blueberries, sprinkle with the sugar and gently stir. Spoon over the mascarpone.

2 To make the topping, rub the butter into the flour and whizz in a food processor until it looks like fine breadcrumbs. Stir in the sugar and lemon zest. Make a well in the centre and tip in the yogurt. Stir until evenly combined, but do not overmix.

3 Spoon the cobbler mixture onto the fruit and mascarpone. Bake for 20 minutes until the topping is risen and golden and the filling is bubbling.

• Per serving 323 kcalories, protein 5g, carbohydrate 49g, fat 13g, saturated fat 8g, fibre 2g, added sugar 17g, salt 0.66g

An unusually light and fluffy cobbler makes an indulgent pudding for Sunday lunch get-togethers.

Plum and Apple Cobbler

750g/1lb 10oz cooking apples
(Bramley's are best), peeled,
cored and stoned
juice of 1 lemon
100g/4oz golden caster sugar
350g/12oz ripe plums, halved,
stoned and quartered

FOR THE COBBLER
100g/4oz self-raising flour
1 tsp cinnamon
50g/2oz butter, cut into small pieces
50g/2oz golden caster sugar
1 egg, beaten
4 tbsp milk
50g/2oz walnut pieces

Takes 50 minutes–1 hour • Serves 4

1 Preheat the oven to 180°C/Gas 4/fan oven 160°C. Butter a 1.5 litre/2¾ pint ovenproof pie dish.
2 Put the apples in a pan with the lemon juice, sugar and 1 tablespoon water. Bring to the boil, then cover and cook gently for 5 minutes. Add the plums and cook for a further 5 minutes.
3 Turn the fruit into the dish. Put the flour and cinnamon in a bowl, add the butter and rub in with your fingertips. Stir in the sugar. Add the egg and milk and mix lightly to a soft batter (this can be done in a food processor).
4 Drop tablespoonfuls of the batter over the fruit, leaving gaps where the fruit peers through. Scatter over the nuts. Bake for 25–30 minutes until the topping is crisp and brown. Serve straight away.

• Per serving 556 kcalories, protein 8g, carbohydrate 90g, fat 21g, saturated fat 8g, fibre 6g, added sugar 37g, salt 0.3g

These flavours are wonderfully sweet,
yet refreshing.

Banana with Tropical Fruit Caramel

juice of 1 large orange
200g/8oz golden caster sugar
4 ripe passion fruit
1 medium-size ripe mango, peeled
and thinly sliced
4 firm large bananas, peeled
finely grated zest and juice of 1 large
lime

Takes 30 minutes • Serves 4

1 In a small pan, bring the orange juice
and 140g/5oz of the sugar slowly to the boil.
Halve the passion fruit and scoop the pulp
into the pan. Stir in the mango slices and
when the mixture has reached boiling point
again, remove the pan from the heat.
2 Slice each banana diagonally into five.
Pour the lime juice over the banana slices
and set aside. Sprinkle the remaining sugar
evenly over the base of a large heavy-based
frying pan. Place the pan over a medium heat
until the sugar has dissolved and turned into
a golden caramel. Toss the bananas into the
pan and leave for 3–4 minutes, turning once.
3 Turn the heat down and stir in the passion
fruit and mango mixture. Heat for a further
2 minutes, then spoon into bowls. Serve
warm with a sprinkling of lime zest.

• Per serving 419 kcalories, protein 10g, carbohydrate
107g, fat none, saturated fat none, fibre 4.1g, added
sugar 59g, salt 0.02g

An irresistible combination, perfect for
cheering up cold winter days.

Baked Plums with Mascarpone

400g tub mascarpone
2 tbsp icing sugar
50g/2oz golden caster sugar
4 clementines
175ml/6fl oz madeira
900g/2lb plums, halved and stoned

Takes 1 hour • Serves 6

1 Preheat the oven to 200°C/Gas 6/fan oven 180°C. Beat the mascarpone and icing sugar until smooth. Put in a serving bowl. Cover. Chill.
2 Tip the caster sugar into a pan, add 300ml/ ½ pint water, the pared zest of one of the clementines and the juice of all four. Slowly bring to the boil and simmer for 5 minutes. Stir in the madeira. Remove from the heat. Arrange the plums in a single layer in a roasting tin, cut side up. Drizzle with the madeira syrup. Bake, uncovered, for 10–12 minutes until just tender.
3 Lift the plums out of the cooking liquid with a slotted spoon and put them in a serving dish. Put the roasting tin on the hob, bring the liquid to the boil and simmer until lightly syrupy – about 10 minutes. Pour the syrup over the plums, leaving the zest behind in the tin. Serve warm, with the mascarpone.

• Per serving 457 kcalories, protein 3g, carbohydrate 35g, fat 31g, saturated fat 19g, fibre 3g, added sugar 14g, salt 0.19g

If you have any leftovers, serve cold with mugs of tea.
But it does only keep for a few days because it's so fruity.

Pear, Hazelnut and Chocolate Cake

175g/6oz butter, cut into small pieces, plus extra for greasing
100g/4oz blanched hazelnuts
140g/5oz self-raising flour
140g/5oz golden caster sugar
2 large eggs, beaten
5 small ripe Conference pears
50g/2oz dark chocolate, chopped into small chunks
2 tbsp apricot jam
single cream, to serve

Takes 1½ hours • Serves 8

1 Preheat the oven to 160°C/Gas 3/fan oven 140°C. Butter and line the base of a 20cm/8in round cake tin. Grind the hazelnuts in a food processor until fairly fine. Mix in the flour. Add the butter and pulse until it forms crumbs. Tip in the sugar and eggs and mix briefly.

2 Peel, core and chop two of the pears. Stir the pears and chocolate lightly into the cake mixture. Spoon the mixture into the prepared tin and smooth the top.

3 Peel, core and slice the remaining pears and scatter over the top of the cake. Press down lightly and bake for 50–60 minutes, until firm to the touch. Cool in the tin for 10 minutes, then turn out and cool on a wire rack. Warm the jam and brush over the top of the cake. Serve warm with cream.

• Per serving 470 kcalories, protein 6g, carbohydrate 47g, fat 30g, saturated fat 14g, fibre 3g, added sugar 18g, salt 0.5g

Easy and utterly delicious –
it will fast become a family favourite.

Choccy Pud

100g/4oz butter or margarine, plus extra for the bowl
2 tbsp golden syrup
100g/4oz dark muscovado sugar
150ml/¼ pint milk
1 egg (large or medium)
1 heaped tbsp cocoa powder
225g/8oz self-raising flour, minus 1 heaped tbsp
1 tsp ground cinnamon
¼ tsp bicarbonate of soda

FOR THE CHOCOLATE SAUCE
4 tbsp milk
4 tbsp cream
1 tbsp golden syrup
100g/4oz good-quality dark chocolate, broken into pieces

Takes 1½ hours • Serves 6

1 Butter a 1.2 litre/2 pint pudding bowl and line the base with a disc of buttered greaseproof paper.

2 Melt the butter, syrup and sugar in a saucepan. Remove from the heat and stir in the milk and egg. Add the cocoa to the flour, then tip this mixture into the pan with the cinnamon and soda. Pour the mixture into the pudding bowl, cover tightly with foil and steam for 1¼ hours.

3 Just before the end, heat the sauce ingredients until melted, stirring all the time. Turn the pudding out (run a knife around the inside of the bowl if necessary) and discard the paper disc. Pour the sauce over the top and serve immediately.

• Per serving 472 kcalories, protein 4g, carbohydrate 50g, fat 30g, saturated fat 14g, fibre 2.5g, added sugar none, salt 0.9g

With their coconut and rum flavours and cooked in individual ramekins, these little cakes are a great modern take on a retro classic.

Little Upside-down Cakes

100g/4oz butter, plus extra
for greasing
100g/4oz light muscovado sugar
2 tbsp dark rum
432g can pineapple rings, drained
6 glacé cherries
cream or custard, to serve

FOR THE CAKE
50g/2oz unsweetened desiccated
coconut
100g/4oz butter, at room temperature
200g/8oz golden caster sugar
3 large eggs
175g/6oz plain flour
1 tsp baking powder
2 tsp vanilla extract
125ml/4fl oz milk

Takes 40 minutes • Serves 6

1 Preheat the oven to 180°C/Gas 4/fan oven 160°C. Butter six 200ml/7fl oz ramekin dishes. For the topping, put the butter, sugar and rum in a pan and heat for 2 minutes until the sugar has melted, stirring occasionally. Carefully pour a little of the mixture into the bottom of each ramekin, then put a pineapple slice with a cherry inside on top.

2 Make the cake. Put the coconut in a pan over a gentle heat, stirring often, until it begins to turn light golden brown, then remove from the heat and leave to cool.

3 Mix it together with all the remaining cake ingredients until they're well combined. Spoon over the pineapple slices, place the ramekins on a baking sheet and bake for 20 minutes, until well risen. Turn out and serve with cream or custard.

• Per serving 696 kcalories, protein 8g, carbohydrate 87g, fat 36g, saturated fat 23g, fibre 2g, added sugar 54g, salt 1.22g

The perfect pud to serve after a winter roast –
just make sure you leave enough room!

Mango and Maple Pudding

FOR THE PUDDING
100g/4oz butter, softened, plus extra
100g/4oz light muscovado sugar
2 eggs, beaten
grated zest of 1 orange and
2–3 tbsp juice
175g/6oz self-raising flour

FOR THE TOPPING
1 ripe medium-sized mango
25g/1oz light muscovado sugar
50g/2oz butter, softened
2 tbsp maple syrup, plus extra to serve
25g/1oz pecan halves

FOR THE MANGO CREAM
1 ripe medium-sized mango
1 tbsp maple syrup
284ml carton whipping cream

Takes 40 minutes, plus 2 hours
steaming • Serves 6–8

1 Butter a 1.4 litre/2½ pint pudding basin. Chop the mango flesh for the topping. Pat dry. Beat the sugar, butter and syrup. Add the nuts and a third of the mango. Spoon into the basin.
2 Make the pudding. Beat the butter and sugar until light and creamy. Add the eggs a little at a time, beating well, then the orange zest. With a metal spoon, fold in the flour a third at a time. Fold in the mango left from the topping and enough orange juice for a soft dropping consistency. Spoon the mixture over the topping and level. Cover tightly, then steam for 2 hours until risen and firm.
3 Chop and mash the mango flesh for the mango cream. Add the syrup. Softly whisk the cream. Swirl the mango into the cream. Turn the pudding out. Pour over more maple syrup. Serve with the mango cream.

• Per serving for six 682 kcalories, protein 7g, carbohydrate 66g, fat 45g, saturated fat 25.5g, fibre 4.1g, added sugar 25.7g, salt 0.77g

Serve with brandy cream or butter
for a real Christmas treat.

Classic Christmas Pudding

1 whole nutmeg (you'll use
three-quarters of it)
2 large Bramley cooking apples,
peeled, cored and chopped
50g/2oz blanched almonds,
chopped
200g box candied peel (in large
pieces), chopped
1kg/2lb 4oz raisins
140g/5oz plain flour
100g/4oz soft fresh white
breadcrumbs
100g/4oz light muscovado sugar
3 large eggs
2 tbsp brandy or cognac, plus extra
for serving
250g packet firm butter, plus extra
for greasing

Takes 45–55 minutes, plus 9 hours
cooking • Makes two 1.2 litre/
2 pint puddings (each serves 8)

1 Grate three-quarters of the nutmeg. Mix all
the ingredients for the pudding, except the
butter, in a large bowl. Holding the butter in
its wrapper, grate a quarter of it into the bowl.
Stir. Repeat until all the butter is grated, then
stir for 3–4 minutes.
2 Generously butter two 1.2 litre/2 pint bowls
and line the bases. Pack in the pudding
mixture. Cover tightly and steam for 8 hours,
topping up with water as necessary. Remove
from the pans. Cool overnight. Re-wrap.
Store in a cool, dry place until Christmas.
3 To serve, boil the pudding for 1 hour.
Unwrap and turn out. Warm 3–4 tablespoons
brandy in a small pan, pour over the pudding
and set light to it.

• Per serving 550 kcalories, protein 5g, carbohydrate
77g, fat 25g, saturated fat 6g, fibre 2g, added sugar
16g, salt 0.92g

If you can't find blueberries, try raspberries and redcurrants,
or chopped strawberries.

Blueberry and Lime Cheesecake

300g/10oz Hobnobs (try the
Caramel and Nut flavour),
crushed
100g/4oz butter, melted
500g/1lb 2oz blueberries
225g/8oz golden caster sugar
finely grated zest and juice of
2 limes
2 × 250g tubs Quark
284ml carton double cream
284ml carton soured cream
4 tsp powdered gelatine, dissolved
in a cup with 3 tablespoons
cold water, standing in a pan
of water over a low heat

Takes 50 minutes, plus cooling
and chilling • Serves 8

1 Preheat the oven to 180°C/Gas 4/fan oven 160°C. Line the base of a 23cm/9in springform tin. Mix the biscuits and butter. Press over the tin's base. Bake for 10 minutes. Cool. In a pan briefly cook one-third of the blueberries with 3 tablespoons water, 175g/6oz of sugar and the zest of 1 lime until the berries burst. Cool. Strain the juice into a pan. Reserve with the berries.
2 Whizz the Quark, both creams, the remaining sugar, lime zest and all the juice. Beat a little creamy mix with the gelatine, then beat into the rest of the mix. Lightly ripple the cooled berries into the creamy mix. Spoon onto the base. Chill to set for about 4 hours.
3 Cook the reserved juice for 2–3 minutes until lightly syrupy. Stir in the uncooked berries. Cool. Slide the cake onto a plate. Top with the syrupy berries.

• Per serving 689 kcalories, protein 16g, carbohydrate 63g, fat 44g, saturated fat 26g, fibre 1g, added sugar 37g, salt 0.75g

The perfect, almost-instant dessert for
a cosy, special dinner for two.

Berry Cheesecake in a Glass

150g punnet of blackberries
1 tbsp golden caster sugar
finely grated zest and juice of
1 lemon
4 gingernut biscuits, crushed
knob of butter, melted
2 tbsp icing sugar
½ × 250g tub mascarpone or
ricotta

Takes 20 minutes • Serves 2

1 Toss the blackberries, caster sugar and 1 tablespoon of the lemon juice in a small pan. Heat gently for 3–4 minutes or until the berries start to burst. Leave to cool.
2 Meanwhile, mix together the crushed biscuits and melted butter. Spoon into two glasses.
3 Gently fold the rest of the lemon juice, the lemon zest and the icing sugar into the mascarpone or ricotta. Divide the lemony cheese between the glasses, then spoon over the blackberries and their syrupy juices. Serve.

• Per serving 497 kcalories, protein 3g, carbohydrate 44g, fat 35g, saturated fat 21g, fibre 3g, added sugar 24g, salt 0.67g

Ideal for a girls' night in – try serving them with
a glass of rosé wine or pink champagne.

Blush Meringues

4 egg whites
edible pink food colouring
200g/8oz caster sugar

FOR THE FILLING
250g/9oz tub mascarpone
284ml carton double cream
1 tbsp icing sugar
couple of handfuls of fresh or frozen
(thawed) mixed berries, lightly
crushed

Takes 2 hours •
Makes 9 filled meringues

1 Preheat the oven to 140°C/Gas 1/fan oven 120°C. Line two baking sheets with parchment. Whisk the egg whites and a generous touch of pink colouring, until stiff. Continue whisking as you sprinkle in the sugar, a tablespoon at a time, then whisk until the mixture is thick and glossy.

2 Using two tablespoons, make 18 large 'quenelle' shapes, spaced well apart on the baking sheets. Bake for about 1½ hours until they are crisp and peel easily from the lining. Cool in the oven for 30 minutes with the door slightly ajar.

3 Beat the mascarpone until smooth. Pour in the cream, add the sugar and whisk to soft peaks. Stir in the fruit lightly so it's rippled through the cream. Sandwich the meringues together with fruit cream. Eat straight away.

• Per filled meringue 380 kcalories, protein 3g, carbohydrate 25g, fat 30g, saturated fat 19g, fibre none, added sugar 24g, salt 0.3g

This is delicious served with waffles
or wafers on the side.

Blackberry Crumble Ice Cream

500g/1lb 2oz blackberries
3 tbsp golden caster sugar
284ml carton double cream
500g carton fresh custard
1 tsp vanilla extract

FOR THE CRUMBLE
50g/2oz porridge oats
50g/2oz butter, melted
50g/2oz light muscovado sugar

Takes about 1 hour • Serves 6

1 Gently heat the blackberries and caster sugar in a pan until the juices start to run. Cover and gently cook for 5–8 minutes until soft. Press through a sieve into a bowl. Chill.
2 Softly whip the cream in a large bowl. Stir in the custard and vanilla. Transfer to an ice cream maker. Process until softly set.
3 Meanwhile, preheat the oven to 180°C/Gas 4/fan oven 160°C. Combine the crumble ingredients and spread over a small baking dish lined with parchment. Bake for 8–10 minutes until pale brown. Cool briefly. Break into small pieces. Cool completely. When softly set, sprinkle the ice cream with half the crumble and half the sauce. Swirl. Freeze until firm.
4 To serve, transfer the ice cream to the fridge for 30 minutes. Sprinkle with the remaining crumble and serve with the remaining sauce.

• Per serving 489 kcalories, protein 6g, carbohydrate 42g, fat 34g, saturated fat 21g, fibre 3g, added sugar 22g, salt 0.39g

Serve these as they are, or with crème fraîche
or a good-quality vanilla ice cream.

Peaches Poached in Rosé Wine

1 bottle good quality rosé wine
140g/5oz golden caster sugar
1 vanilla pod, split in half lengthways
6 ripe but firm peaches
6 tbsp framboise (raspberry liqueur)

Takes 50 minutes–1 hour • Serves 6

1 Pour the wine into a saucepan, then tip in the sugar and add the split vanilla pod. Slowly bring the wine to the boil, stirring to dissolve the sugar, then boil for 5 minutes. Turn down the heat, then add the peaches, cover and poach them very gently for about 10 minutes or until tender. If the peaches aren't completely submerged in the syrup, turn them over gently to poach them evenly.

2 Lift the peaches out of the syrup with a slotted spoon and carefully slip off their skins. Leave to cool in a shallow bowl.

3 Meanwhile, bring the syrup to a rolling boil and boil for about 10 minutes or until it's well reduced, thick and syrupy, but still pourable. Let the syrup cool slightly then stir in the liqueur and pour it over the peaches. Serve warm or chilled.

• Per serving 253 kcalories, protein 1g, carbohydrate 41g, fat none, saturated fat none, fibre 2g, added sugar 29g, salt 0.02g

Here mascarpone is used instead of the traditional custard,
giving a clean, Italian flavour – simply heavenly!

Italian Apricot Fool

500g/1lb 2oz ripe fresh apricots,
halved and stoned
finely grated zest and juice of
1 lemon
140g/5oz golden caster sugar
3 tbsp Cointreau or other orange
flavoured liqueur
500g carton mascarpone
142ml carton double cream
18 amaretti biscuits, plus extra
to serve

Takes 30–40 minutes, plus cooling •
Serves 6

1 Put the apricot halves in a saucepan with the lemon zest and juice and the sugar. Shake the pan to combine, then simmer, uncovered, over a medium heat until the apricots are soft – about 10–15 minutes.

2 Tip the contents of the pan into a blender or food processor and whizz to a purée. Decant into a bowl, stir in the liqueur and leave to cool – about 20–30 minutes.

3 Soften the mascarpone in its tub by whisking it vigorously with a fork. Whip the cream in a bowl to soft peaks. Fold in the mascarpone with a large metal spoon, then lightly swirl in the apricot purée. Spoon the mixture into six wine glasses. (They'll keep in the fridge for up to a day.) To serve, crumble over the amaretti, with a few on the side for dunking.

• Per serving 633 kcalories, protein 4g, carbohydrate 39g, fat 50g, saturated fat 31g, fibre 1g, added sugar 27g, salt 0.27g

Serve warm or cold with a glass of rosé wine.

Baked Nectarines with Honeyed Almonds

6–8 ripe nectarines
50g/2oz flaked almonds
2 tbsp runny honey
2 tbsp golden caster sugar
8 tbsp French Muscat wine, such as
Rivesaltes or Beaumes de Venise

FOR THE ALMOND CREAM
284ml carton whipping cream
1 tbsp golden caster sugar
dash almond-flavoured liqueur

Takes 40 minutes • Serves 6

1 Preheat the oven to 200°C/Gas 6/fan oven 180°C. Cut the nectarines in half through the dimple line and remove the stones. Nestle the halved nectarines, cut-side up, in a single layer in a shallow ovenproof dish.
2 Mix the flaked almonds and honey in a bowl. Place a teaspoonful of the almonds in the cavity of each nectarine half. Sprinkle the sugar over. Carefully spoon the muscat into the dish. Bake, uncovered, for 20 minutes, switch off the oven and leave to 'cook' for another 10 minutes until the fruit is tender. Remove from the oven.
3 To make the almond cream, beat the cream with the sugar and liqueur until thickened. Spoon into a bowl and serve with the baked nectarines.

• Per serving 336 kcalories, protein 4g, carbohydrate 25g, fat 23g, saturated fat 12g, fibre 2g, added sugar 12g, salt 0.06g

If you're lucky enough to have any left over, this wonderfully moist cake is fantastic with coffee the next morning.

Raspberry and Amaretti Crunch Cake

175g/6oz soft butter, plus extra for greasing
175g/6oz golden caster sugar
3 eggs
140g/5oz self-raising flour
85g/3oz ground almonds
140g/5oz amaretti biscuits, roughly broken
250g punnet raspberries

TO SERVE
icing sugar, to dust
142ml carton single cream

Takes 1½ hours • Serves 6

1 Preheat the oven to 160°C/Gas 3/fan oven 140°C. Butter and line the base of a loose-bottomed 20cm/8in round cake tin. Beat the butter, caster sugar, eggs, flour and ground almonds in a large bowl. Spread half the cake mixture in the lined tin. Scatter over half of the amaretti biscuits, then a third of the raspberries. Very lightly press into the cake mixture.

2 Dollop spoonfuls of the remaining cake mixture over the amaretti and raspberries and spread evenly. Scatter the remaining amaretti and half the remaining raspberries over the top. Bake for 55–60 minutes, until a skewer inserted into the centre comes out clean.

3 Cool for 15 minutes in the tin. Run a knife round the edge and turn out. Serve warm or cooled, lightly dusted with icing sugar, with the remaining raspberries and single cream.

• Per serving 640 kcalories, protein 12g, carbohydrate 68g, fat 37g, saturated fat 17g, fibre 4g, added sugar 34g, salt 0.92g

The perfect crumbly dessert for a
Sunday lunch or dinner.

Strawberry and Cinnamon Torte

175g/6oz ground almonds
175g/6oz butter, softened
175g/6oz golden caster sugar
175g/6oz self-raising flour
1 tsp ground cinnamon
1 egg, plus 1 egg yolk
450g/1lb strawberries, hulled and
sliced
icing sugar, for dusting
whipped double cream mixed with
Greek yogurt, to serve

Takes 1¼ hours • Serves 6–8

1 Preheat the oven to 180°C/Gas 4/fan
oven 160°C. Butter and line the base
of a loose-bottomed 23cm/9in cake tin.
In a food processor, mix the ground almonds,
butter, sugar, flour, cinnamon, egg and egg
yolk until evenly mixed.
2 Tip half the mixture in the tin and smooth.
Spread the strawberries on top. Top with the
remaining cake mixture. Spread smooth.
3 Bake for 1 hour–1 hour 5 minutes. Check
after 40 minutes – if the torte is getting too
brown, cover loosely with foil. When cooked,
the torte should be slightly risen and dark
golden brown.
4 Cool slightly, then remove from the tin.
Slide on to a plate and dust with icing sugar.
Serve warm, in wedges, with spoonfuls of
cream and Greek yogurt.

• Per serving for eight 491 kcalories, protein 9g,
carbohydrate 45g, fat 32g, saturated fat 13g, fibre 3g,
added sugar 23g, salt 0.68g

Crème brûlée is a popular dinner-party dessert,
and easier to make than you think.

Blackberry Crème Brûlées

200g/8oz blackberries
5 tbsp golden caster sugar
284ml carton double cream
4 tbsp milk
3 medium egg yolks, whisked
50ml miniature (or 3 tbsp) Baileys or
1 tsp vanilla extract

TO FINISH
6 tbsp golden caster sugar
a few extra blackberries

Takes 1½ hours, plus cooling and
overnight chilling • Serves 6

1 Preheat the oven to 140°C/Gas 1/fan oven 120°C. Gently cook the blackberries and 1 tablespoon of the sugar in a pan for 1–2 minutes until the fruit begins to give up its juice. Spoon into six ramekins (150ml/¼ pint size). Put them in a roasting tin.
2 Bring the cream and milk to a boil in a pan, then slowly whisk into the egg yolks. Whisk in the remaining sugar and the Baileys or vanilla. Strain custard into a jug, then pour over the fruit. Pour boiling water into the tin to come halfway up the sides of the ramekins. Bake for 40 minutes until the centres are just wobbly.
3 Take from the oven, leave to stand in the water for 10 minutes. Remove, cool and chill overnight. Sprinkle the tops of each evenly with caster sugar and caramelise using a blowtorch. Serve with extra berries.

• Per serving 415 kcalories, protein 3g, carbohydrate 34g, fat 30g, saturated fat 15.1g, fibre 1.2g, added sugar 30.8g, salt 0.07g

A dessert to impress your friends. The saffron adds zest, a seductive aroma and a stylish note.

Poached Saffron Pears

generous pinch of saffron
100g/4oz golden caster sugar
5 tbsp ginger wine
1 star anise
1 strip orange peel (pared with a peeler)
4 medium Conference pears, peeled, stalks left on
mascarpone, to serve

Takes 45 minutes, plus chilling • Serves 4

1 Soak the saffron in 6 tablespoons warm water and leave for 1 hour to infuse. Put the sugar in a medium pan with 175ml/6fl oz water and the ginger wine. Heat slowly to dissolve the sugar, stirring, then turn up the heat and boil for 3–4 minutes. Add the star anise and orange peel.

2 Lower the heat and add the pears. Press scrunched greaseproof paper lightly over them, cover and simmer for 30 minutes, turning occasionally. Remove and transfer to a bowl. Strain the syrup into a jug and stir in the soaked saffron and liquid. Pour over the pears, cover and chill for 24 hours, turning once.

3 Serve each pear drizzled with a little syrup, with dollops of mascarpone.

• Per serving 199 kcalories, protein 1g, carbohydrate 46g, fat 1g, saturated fat none, fibre 3g, added sugar 26g, salt 0.03g

Rich with brandy-steeped prunes, this is a cake
for real lovers of chocolate.

Prune and Chocolate Torte

250g/9oz no-soak prunes, halved
4 tbsp brandy
25g/1oz cocoa powder
100g/4oz dark chocolate (at least
70% cocoa solids), broken
into pieces
50g/2oz butter
175g/6oz golden caster sugar
4 large egg whites
85g/3oz plain flour
1 tsp ground cinnamon
lightly whipped cream or crème
fraîche, to serve

Takes 1 hour 5 minutes,
plus 30 minutes soaking • Serves 8

1 Soak the prunes in brandy for about
30 minutes. Preheat the oven to 190ºC/
Gas 5/fan oven 170ºC. Butter a 23cm/9in
loose-bottomed cake tin. Put the cocoa,
chocolate, butter and 140g/5oz of the sugar
in a pan, add 100ml/3½fl oz hot water and
gently heat until smooth. Leave to cool slightly.
2 Whisk the egg whites to soft peaks, then
gradually whisk in the remaining sugar. Sift
the flour and cinnamon over and gently fold in
with a metal spoon, until almost combined.
Add the chocolate mixture and fold in until
evenly combined.
3 Pour the mixture into the tin and arrange
the prunes over the top. Sprinkle over
any remaining brandy and bake for about
30 minutes until just firm. Serve with cream
or crème fraîche.

• Per serving 311 kcalories, protein 5g, carbohydrate
51g, fat 10g, saturated fat 6g, fibre 3g, added sugar
31g, salt 0.18g

Always a popular pudding,
but such a simple method!

Hot Chocolate Soufflés

butter, for greasing
2 tbsp ground almonds
150g bar dark chocolate, broken
into pieces
4 tbsp strong black coffee,
Tia Maria or Frangelico
2 tsp plain flour
100g/4oz golden caster sugar
4 eggs, separated
good vanilla ice cream, to serve

FOR THE SAUCE
142ml carton double cream
100g/4oz dark chocolate, broken
into pieces
2 tbsp strong black coffee,
Tia Maria or Frangelico

Takes 1 hour • Serves 6

1 Preheat the oven to 190°C/Gas 5/fan oven 170°C. Butter six 200ml/7fl oz ramekin dishes. Dust the insides with ground almonds. Melt the chocolate with the coffee or liqueur. Stir until smooth. Cool slightly. Stir the flour, half the sugar and the egg yolks into the melted chocolate. Whisk the egg whites to soft peaks. Whisk in the remaining sugar, until the mix is thick. Gently fold into the chocolate mixture in four batches. Divide between the ramekins.
2 Bake for 15–25 minutes until risen and the crusts feel firm.
3 Meanwhile, make the sauce. Heat the cream in a small pan. When it simmers, remove from the heat and stir in the chocolate until smooth. Stir in the coffee or liqueur. Split the tops of the soufflés open, add a scoop of ice cream and a drizzle of sauce, and serve.

• Per serving 503 kcalories, protein 10g, carbohydrate 39g, fat 35g, saturated fat 17g, fibre 3g, added sugar 28g, salt 0.17g

The citrus syrup makes this cake wonderfully moist.
Serve with yogurt or crème fraîche, and orange segments.

Orange and Saffron Syrup Cake

200ml/7fl oz light olive oil, plus extra
for greasing
100g/4oz skinned hazelnuts, ground
50g/2oz semolina or polenta
175g/6oz golden caster sugar
1½ tsp baking powder
2 large oranges
4 medium eggs
generous pinch of saffron threads
85g/3oz icing sugar

Takes 1 hour • Serves 8

1 Preheat the oven to 180°C/Gas 4/fan oven 160°C. Oil the base of a 23cm/9in ring tin. Toss the ground hazelnuts in a frying pan over a medium heat, stirring frequently, until brown. Cool, then mix with the semolina or polenta, caster sugar and baking powder.
2 Finely grate the zest from one orange and combine with the eggs and oil. Beat well, then fold into the dry ingredients. Pour into the tin. Bake for 30–40 minutes until done.
3 Meanwhile, pare the zest from the other orange and thinly shred. Put in a saucepan with the juice from both oranges, the saffron and icing sugar. Bring to the boil, then simmer gently for 5 minutes.
4 When the cake is done, cool in the tin slightly, then turn out onto a plate. While warm, skewer the cake and spoon the syrup over.

• Per serving 455 kcalories, protein 7g, carbohydrate 43g, fat 30g, saturated fat 4g, fibre 2g, added sugar 33g, salt 0.4g

Time the cooking carefully to get the insides nice and gooey. But don't panic about serving them straight away as they're good warm or cool.

Light and Dark Choc Puds

100g/4oz butter, chopped, plus extra for greasing
50g/2oz plain flour, plus extra for dusting
100g bar dark chocolate, broken into pieces
3 eggs
85g/3oz golden caster sugar
8–10 squares of milk chocolate
Maldon sea salt flakes (optional)

Takes 25 minutes • Serves 6

1 Preheat the oven to 200°C/Gas 6/fan oven 180°C. Butter and lightly flour six 150ml/1¼ pint ramekins.

2 Melt the dark chocolate and butter in a bowl in the microwave for 2–3 minutes on Medium, stirring halfway through. Whisk the eggs and sugar until the mixture leaves a trail on the top when the whisk blades are lifted. Stir in the flour, then the melted chocolate mix. Divide between the ramekins and push 1 or 2 squares of milk chocolate into the centre of each. Put on a baking sheet and bake for 12 minutes exactly.

3 Cool for 5 minutes, then turn out onto plates and sprinkle each with a pinch of sea salt, if you like. They are good eaten warm or at room temperature.

• Per serving 396 kcalories, protein 7g, carbohydrate 34g, fat 27g, saturated fat 15g, fibre 1g, added sugar 24g, salt 0.39g

Great for lovers of ice cream and when you want a dessert that looks like Christmas pudding but is altogether different.

Iced Berry Pud

284ml carton double cream
500g carton good-quality ready-made custard
100g/4oz golden caster sugar
100ml/3½fl oz dark rum, plus 1 tbsp extra
170g packet dried berries and cherries (or same weight mix of dried cranberries, cherries, blueberries and raisins)
sprigs of sugar-frosted bay leaves and little bunches of sugar-frosted red and green grapes, to decorate

Takes 20–30 minutes, plus 2½ hours chilling and cooling and overnight freezing • Serves 6–8

1 Softly whip the cream and stir in the custard. Put in the freezer for 1½ hours, until starting to freeze around the edges.
2 Meanwhile, put the sugar in a pan with 100ml/3½fl oz rum. Heat slowly until the sugar has dissolved, tip in the fruits, and simmer gently for 1 minute. Pour everything into a wide bowl (so it cools quickly), and leave for about an hour until cold. Add the extra rum for a bit more kick.
3 Stir the cream and custard with a balloon whisk to break it up. Stir in the cooled fruit. Pour into a 1.2 litre/2 pint pudding basin, cover and freeze overnight until firm.
4 To serve, dip the basin quickly into boiling water, go round the sides with a knife, then turn the pudding out onto a plate. Decorate with clusters of frosted bay leaves and grapes.

• Per serving for eight 385 kcalories, protein 3g, carbohydrate 44g, fat 20g, saturated fat 13g, fibre 1g, added sugar 19g, salt 0.17g

Exotic passion fruit gives this fresh take on
a traditional pudding the wow-factor.

Passion Fruit Trifle

250g tub mascarpone
50g/2oz golden caster sugar
1 tsp vanilla extract
284ml carton double cream
9 passion fruit
juice 1 orange
3 thick slices brioche loaf or plain
sponge cake
3 peaches, stoned and thinly sliced

Takes 25 minutes • Serves 6

1 Beat the mascarpone, sugar and vanilla until smooth. In a separate bowl, whisk the double cream until softly whipped. Fold the mascarpone mix into the whipped cream. Set aside.

2 Cut 8 passion fruit in half, scoop the pulp into a small bowl and stir in the orange juice. Slice the crusts off the brioche or cake and quarter each slice.

3 Lay the brioche or cake in the bottom of a glass bowl. Top with half of the passion fruit pulp and half of the peach slices, then spoon over half of the mascarpone cream. Repeat the layers once more (keeping a few peach slices back), topping off with a layer of mascarpone. Use the pulp from the last passion fruit and the reserved peach slices to decorate.

• Per serving 553 kcalories, protein 5g, carbohydrate 30g, fat 47g, saturated fat 28g, fibre 2g, added sugar 10g, salt 0.36g

With only five ingredients, this is a great little number to have up your sleeve when you're in a hurry.

Lemon and Raspberry Baskets

50g/2oz dark chocolate, broken into pieces
325g jar good-quality lemon curd
350ml half-fat crème fraîche
150g punnet raspberries
6 brandy snap baskets

Takes 10 minutes • Serves 6

1 Melt the chocolate in the microwave for 2 minutes on High, stirring halfway through. Meanwhile, stir together the lemon curd and the crème fraîche.

2 Divide half the raspberries between the baskets, spoon over the lemon cream and top with the rest of the berries.

3 Drizzle the dark chocolate over the tops of the baskets and leave in the fridge to set for 5–10 minutes or up to 1 hour – no longer or they will soften.

• Per serving 348 kcalories, protein 3g, carbohydrate 52g, fat 16g, saturated fat 8g, fibre 1g, added sugar 29g, salt 0.23g

Deceptively creamy but low in fat, these no-cook raspberry pots take just a few minutes to assemble.

Crushed Raspberry Creams

50g/2oz golden caster sugar
2 × 125g punnets raspberries
200g tub half-fat crème fraîche
150g tub fat-free Greek yogurt
3 meringue shells, either bought or homemade, broken into large pieces

Takes 10 minutes • Serves 4

1 In a small bowl stir a sprinkling of the sugar in with the raspberries, crushing them very slightly as you stir, but still leaving them more or less whole.

2 In a separate bowl, fold the crème fraîche and yogurt together with the remaining sugar and the meringue pieces.

3 Divide the raspberries among four small glasses and top with the creamy meringue mixture. The raspberry pots can be eaten straight away or will keep in the fridge for up to 4 hours.

• Per serving 214 kcalories, protein 7g, carbohydrate 31g, fat 8g, saturated fat 5g, fibre 2g, added sugar 25g, salt 0.23g

This is a really refreshing, palate-cleansing iced dessert –
perfect for a hot, sunny day. And it contains absolutely no fat!

Lemon Ice and Minty Strawberries

2 unwaxed lemons, each chopped
into eight
140g/5oz golden caster sugar
400g/14oz strawberries, hulled
and sliced
small handful of mint leaves,
roughly chopped

Takes 30 minutes, plus freezing •
Serves 4

1 For the lemon ice, tip the lemons into a blender with the sugar and 500ml/18fl oz water. Blitz for a minute or two until the lemon is chopped to a pulp. Strain the juice into a shallowish freezer container, pressing down on the lemon pulp with the back of a spoon to release its flavour. Discard the pulp.

2 Reserve 2 tablespoons of the juice in a bowl. Cover the rest with cling film and freeze for 4 hours or until firm. When it's frozen, break it into chunks and tip it back into the blender. Blitz until it's a smooth sorbet consistency. Tip it back into the freezer container and freeze for another 30 minutes to firm up.

3 While the ice is freezing, toss the strawberries and mint in the reserved lemon juice. When the ice is scoopable, spoon it into bowls and top with the strawberries.

• Per serving 174 kcalories, protein 1g, carbohydrate 44g, fat none, saturated fat none, fibre 1g, added sugar 37g, salt 1.3g

Turn fresh summer berries into a stylish but simple dessert
with a flavoured syrup.

Summer Fruits with Lemon Syrup

100g/4oz golden caster sugar
1 lemongrass stalk
2 strips lemon zest (peeled with
a vegetable peeler)
500g/1lb 2oz mixed summer fruits,
such as strawberries, raspberries
and redcurrants

Takes 10 minutes, plus steeping •
Serves 4

1 Stir 250ml/9fl oz boiling water and the
sugar together until the sugar has dissolved.
2 Bruise the lemongrass with a rolling pin
to release the flavour, then add to the syrup
with the lemon zest. Leave to cool. (This can
keep in a jar in the fridge for 2–3 days.)
3 Pour the syrup over the fruit, stir to mix,
then leave to steep for about 30 minutes
before serving.

• Per serving 130 kcalories, protein 1g, carbohydrate
33g, fat none, saturated fat none, fibre 2.7g, added
sugar 26.3g, salt 0.02g

If you have a gluten or wheat intolerance, try these individual summer puddings made with gluten-free bread.

Summer Puddings

250g punnet strawberries, hulled and halved
125g punnet blueberries
125g punnet blackberries
85g/3oz golden caster sugar
6 thin slices of bread from a gluten-free loaf

Takes 30 minutes, plus chilling • Serves 4

1 Put the strawberries into a large saucepan with the other fruit, sugar and 3 tablespoons water over a low heat for 2–3 minutes until the juice runs from the fruit. Remove from the heat.
2 Using biscuit cutters, stamp out four 5.5cm/ 2¼in circles from the bread, then use a 7cm/ 2¾in cutter for another four circles. Put the smaller circles into the base of four 175ml/ 6fl oz pudding basins.
3 Spoon in the fruit, then top with the larger circles. Press down, then spoon over just enough juice to colour the bread red. Cover with cling film and put a weight (such as a jar of jam) on top. Refrigerate for at least 4 hours, or overnight. Reserve the remaining juice.
4 To serve, uncover the puddings and run a knife around the edge. Invert each one onto a serving plate. Spoon the reserved juices over.

• Per serving 212 kcalories, protein 1g, carbohydrate 52g, fat 1g, saturated fat none, fibre 2g, added sugar 22g, salt 0.53g

This is an easy, no-fuss cherry and lemon
version of the classic French recipe.

Cheat's Clafoutis

450g/1lb cherries, pitted
2 tbsp cherry, plum or apricot jam
finely grated zest and juice of
1 lemon
50g/2oz plain flour
3 large eggs
450ml/16fl oz skimmed milk
½ tsp ground cinnamon
3 tbsp golden caster sugar
icing sugar, to dust

Takes 50 minutes • Serves 2

1 Preheat the oven to 190°C/gas 5/fan oven 170°C. Lightly oil a shallow 1.3 litre/2¼ pint baking dish. Gently heat the cherries and jam in a large saucepan, stirring until the jam melts over the cherries. Tip them into the dish and sprinkle with the lemon zest and juice.
2 Whizz the flour, eggs, milk, cinnamon and sugar in a food processor for 30 seconds until smooth. Pour over the cherries.
3 Put the dish on a baking tray and bake for 25–30 minutes or until the custard is set and the jam is beginning to bubble through. Dust with icing sugar and serve hot.

• Per serving 532 kcalories, protein 23g, carbohydrate 92g, fat 11g, saturated fat 3g, fibre 2g, added sugar 38g, salt 0.66g

This pudding is lightning quick and low-fat, too.
For a special treat, serve with oatmeal shortbread biscuits.

Effortless Raspberry Iced Mousse

2 × 250g tubs Quark (low-fat cream
cheese)
50g/2oz icing sugar
squeeze or two of lemon
250g pack frozen raspberries

Takes 5 minutes • Serves 4

1 Tip the Quark and icing sugar into a large bowl, squeeze in a few drops of lemon juice and beat with a wooden spoon until smooth and creamy. (You can do this an hour or two ahead.)

2 Gently stir in the raspberries (straight from the freezer) until they begin to break up and the mixture is streaked pink.

3 Taste and add a little more lemon juice if liked. Spoon into glasses and serve immediately.

• Per serving 158 kcalories, protein 19g, carbohydrate 21g, fat none, saturated fat none, fibre 2g, added sugar 13g, salt 0.17g

This has got to be the fastest dessert ever!
It's delicious with other fruits, too.

Crunch Spiced Rhubarb Trifles

540g can rhubarb, drained
pinch ground ginger
500g tub fresh custard
6 gingernut biscuits, roughly
crushed

Takes 5 minutes • Serves 4

1 Mix the rhubarb and ginger together and divide between four serving glasses.

2 Spoon the custard on top (you will have some left over).

3 Finish with a sprinkling of crushed biscuit and serve.

• Per serving 254 kcalories, protein 5g, carbohydrate 42g, fat 10g, saturated fat 5g, fibre 1g, added sugar 18g, salt 0.3g

Light, frothy and fruity, these puds are smart enough for entertaining.

Pineapple and Banana Custard Meringues

227g can pineapple pieces in natural juice
3 tbsp cornflour
2 large eggs, separated
425ml/¾ pint semi-skimmed milk
1 tsp vanilla extract
50g/2oz golden caster sugar
2 bananas, sliced

Takes 25–35 minutes • Serves 4

1 Preheat the oven to 190°C/Gas 5/fan oven 170°C. Drain the pineapple juice into a medium-sized pan. Stir in the cornflour, then the egg yolks, milk and vanilla. Heat, stirring all the time, until the mixture boils and thickens. Turn the heat to low and cook gently for 1 minute, stirring all the time. Remove the pan from the heat and stir in half the sugar. Tip in the pineapple and bananas and stir together gently. Add a little more sugar if necessary.
2 Spoon the mixture into four individual baking dishes or large ovenproof teacups. Bake on a baking sheet for 5 minutes while you make the topping.
3 Whisk the egg whites until softly stiff. Tip in the remaining sugar and whisk until glossy. Pile onto the hot desserts and bake for 5 more minutes until golden.

• Per serving 259 kcalories, protein 8g, carbohydrate 48g, fat 5g, saturated fat 2g, fibre 1g, added sugar 14g, salt 0.28g

For a special occasion, substitute half the apple juice
with 150ml/¼ pint of red wine.

Poached Pears with Blackberries

4 medium pears
zest of 1 lemon (peel off with a
potato peeler)
1 tbsp lemon juice
250g/9oz blackberries
300ml/½ pint unsweetened apple
juice
50g/2oz golden caster sugar
8 tbsp fat-free natural Greek yogurt

Takes 40 minutes • Serves 4

1 Peel the pears but don't remove their
stalks. Place them in a saucepan with the
lemon zest and juice, half the blackberries,
the apple juice and caster sugar. Heat until
simmering, then cover and cook gently for
20–25 minutes until the pears are tender,
turning them once.
2 Remove the pears from the liquid and
cool for a few minutes. Halve each, core
with a teaspoon or melon baler, and transfer
to four dishes.
3 Strain the liquid through a sieve, into
a pan. Add the remaining blackberries
and warm gently. Serve the pears and
blackberries with the yogurt.

• Per serving 180 kcalories, protein 5g, carbohydrate
41g, fat none, saturated fat none, fibre 5g, added
sugar 13g, salt trace

With only four ingredients, this is a simple and speedy low-fat pudding. Serve with something creamy.

Vanilla-poached Plums

500g/1lb 2oz plums
200g/8oz golden caster sugar
cinnamon stick
vanilla pod, split and seeds
scraped from the middle

Takes 35 minutes • Serves 4

1 Cut the plums into quarters and remove the stones. Tip the sugar into a pan with 225ml/8fl oz water, the cinnamon and vanilla pod and seeds. Gently heat until the sugar dissolves.

2 Slide the fruit into the syrup. Bring the mixture to the boil, then let it simmer for 5–10 minutes, depending on the ripeness, until the plums are soft.

3 Leave to cool slightly, then serve.

• Per serving 239 kcalories, protein 1g, carbohydrate 63g, fat 1g, saturated fat none, fibre 2g, added sugar 53g, salt 0.01g

You'll love the flavours and textures of this healthy,
but creamy Indian dessert.

Creamy Saffron Yogurt

700g/1lb 9oz fat-free Greek yogurt
2 tsp green cardamom pods, seeds
removed
100g/4oz golden caster sugar
8–10 saffron strands
1 tsp milk

TO SERVE
1 tbsp shelled pistachios, slivered
1 large ripe mango, sliced

Takes 35 minutes • Serves 6

1 Place a piece of muslin or thick kitchen paper in a large sieve set over a large bowl. Spoon the yogurt into the sieve, cover with another piece of muslin or 2 sheets of kitchen paper and set aside at room temperature for 25–30 minutes (to remove excess moisture).
2 Crush the cardamom seeds using a pestle and mortar – you will need 1 teaspoon of ground cardamom. Lift off and discard the top layer of muslin or paper from the yogurt, then scrape the yogurt into a bowl and stir in the sugar.
3 Mix the saffron strands with the milk. Add the lot to the yogurt with the ground cardamom. Stir well for a few minutes. Divide between six small glasses and scatter over the pistachios. Serve at room temperature, with fresh mango slices on the side.

• Per serving 133 kcalories, protein 12g, carbohydrate 23g, fat none, saturated fat none, fibre none, added sugar 17.5g, salt 0.21g

These are good with low-fat fromage frais mixed with a little honey.

Spiced Roasted Apples and Blackberries

4 medium Bramley apples, each
weighing about 200g/8oz
4 tbsp runny honey
½ tsp ground cinnamon
finely grated zest and juice of
1 large orange
250g/9oz blackberries

Takes 50 minutes–1 hour • Serves 4

1 Preheat the oven to 180°C/Gas 4/fan oven 160°C. Core the apples so you have a hole the size of a pound coin in each one. Make a cut just into the skin around the middle of each apple.

2 Stand the apples in a shallow baking dish large enough to take all four. Mix together the honey, cinnamon and orange zest, put an equal amount into the cavity of each apple, then pour the orange juice into the dish.

3 Roast the apples for about 40 minutes, spooning the juices over them occasionally. When the apples are almost ready, spoon the blackberries around and over the top of each apple. Return to the oven for 10 minutes or until the juices start to run. Spoon the blackberries and juices over the apples to serve.

• Per serving 129 kcalories, protein 1g, carbohydrate 32g, fat 0.3g, saturated fat none, fibre 5g, added sugar 15g, salt trace

This is a great pudding for making ahead and grilling just before serving.

Prune and Vanilla Brûlée

290g can of pitted Californian prunes
1 tbsp vanilla extract
250g/9oz tub ricotta
500g tub virtually fat-free fromage frais
5 tbsp light muscovado sugar

Takes 15 minutes • Serves 4

1 Tip the prunes and their juice into a bowl and stir in the vanilla extract. Divide the vanilla prunes between four 150ml/¼ pint ramekins.
2 Preheat the grill to high. Mix the ricotta with the fromage frais and stir in 1 tablespoon of the muscovado sugar. Spoon this mixture over the prunes and level the tops. (You can make ahead up to here and store in the fridge for up to 4 hours.)
3 Sprinkle the remaining sugar over the top of the mixture then put the ramekins on to a baking tray. Grill the puddings for 4–5 minutes until the sugar is bubbling nicely and has caramelised. Serve immediately.

• Per serving 287 kcalories, protein 16g, carbohydrate 42g, fat 7g, saturated fat 5g, fibre 1g, added sugar 22g, salt 0.31g

Don't be put off by the black pepper used in this recipe –
it's essential for bringing out the wonderful mulled wine flavours.

Roasted Fruits with Honey Sauce

4 fresh bay leaves
2 cinnamon sticks
1 vanilla pod
4 seeds from ½ star anise
½ tsp freshly ground black pepper
finely grated zest and juice of
3 oranges
4 tbsp runny honey
3 tbsp light muscovado sugar
6 fresh peaches or nectarines,
halved and stoned
25g/1oz unsalted butter
6 fresh figs, halved

Takes 50 minutes • Serves 6

1 Tear the bay leaves and break the cinnamon into two or three pieces to release the oils and perfumes. Split the vanilla pod in half and scrape out the seeds with the back of a knife. Mix with the star anise seeds and the pepper, orange zest and juice, honey and sugar to make a sauce.

2 Preheat the oven to 200°C/Gas 6/fan oven 180°C. Put the peaches or nectarines skin side down in a large baking dish or roasting tray with sides. Pour the spicy sauce over the fruit and dot with the butter.

3 Roast in the oven for 10 minutes, add the figs and baste the fruits with a large spoon. Roast for 15 minutes more, basting at least three times, until the fruits are tender. Serve straight away.

• Per serving 160 kcalories, protein 2g, carbohydrate 32g, fat 4g, saturated fat 2g, fibre 3g, added sugar 15g, salt trace

This recipe tastes so rich and creamy,
no one will believe it isn't high in fat.

Mango and Passion Fruit Roulade

175g/6oz golden caster sugar
3 large egg whites, beaten until doubled in bulk
1 level tsp cornflour
1 tsp malt vinegar
1 tsp vanilla extract
icing sugar, for dusting, plus extra for decorating
200g/8oz fat-free Greek yogurt
1 large ripe mango, peeled, stoned and diced
pulp from 4 passion fruit
a few physalis, to decorate

FOR THE RASPBERRY SAUCE
200g/8oz raspberries (fresh or frozen, thawed)
2 tbsp icing sugar

Takes 1 hour–1 hour 10 minutes • Serves 6

1 Preheat the oven to 150°C/Gas 2/fan oven 130°C. Line a 33 × 23cm/13 × 9in swiss roll tin with parchment. Slowly whisk the caster sugar with the eggs until thick. Mix the cornflour, vinegar and vanilla. Whisk into the egg whites. Spoon into the tin and level the top. Bake for 30 minutes until just firm.
2 Make the sauce. Whizz the raspberries and icing sugar in a blender, then sieve.
3 Remove the meringue. Cover with damp greaseproof paper for 10 minutes. Dust another sheet of greaseproof with icing sugar. Discard the damp paper. Turn the meringue on to the sugar-coated paper. Remove the lining. Spread the yogurt over the meringue. Scatter with the mango and passion fruit. Roll up the roulade from a short end. Decorate with icing sugar and physalis. Serve with the sauce.

• Per serving 223 kcalories, protein 5g, carbohydrate 45g, fat 4g, saturated fat 1g, fibre 2g, added sugar 33g, salt 0.17g

A fabulous low-fat dinner-party dessert to please sorbet fans.

Mango and Raspberry Meringue Shiver

100g/4oz golden caster sugar
2 large, ripe mangoes, peeled and stoned, flesh chopped
juice of 2 limes
2 × 150g fat-free Greek yogurt
140g/5oz raspberries

FOR THE MERINGUES
200g/8oz golden caster sugar
4 egg whites, whisked until stiff
¼ tsp cardamom seeds, crushed
(from about 6 pods)

TO SERVE
2 tbsp icing sugar
140g/5oz raspberries

Takes 2 hours, plus freezing
and defrosting • Serves 12

1 For the sorbet, dissolve the sugar in 100ml/3½fl oz water. Pour into a bowl. Cool. Purée the mango and lime juice until smooth. Stir into the syrup with the yogurt. Churn in an ice cream machine for 15–30 minutes, until softly frozen. Fold in the raspberries and freeze.
2 Preheat the oven to 120°C/Gas 1/fan oven 100°C. Line two baking sheets with parchment. Draw a 20cm/8in circle on each. Whisk 2 tablespoons of the sugar with the eggs. Fold in the rest with the cardamom. Swirl the meringue inside the paper circles. Bake for 1¼–1½ hours until crisp. Cool. Remove the paper.
3 Remove the sorbet from the freezer 2 hours ahead. After 1 hour, scoop the sorbet onto one meringue. Top with the other. Smooth the outside. Freeze for no more than 1 hour. Serve with icing sugar and raspberries.

• Per serving 149 kcalories, protein 4g, carbohydrate 35g, fat 1g, saturated fat none, fibre 2g, added sugar 25g, salt 0.11g

Index

Picture credits and recipe credits

BBC Worldwide would like to thank the following for providing photographs. While every effort has been made to trace and acknowledge all photographers, we would like to apologize should there be any errors or omissions.

Marie-Louise Avery p143; Iain Bagwell p19, p43, p45, p197; Steve Baxter p31, p121; Martin Brigdale p47, p119, p175; Linda Burgess p117; Pete Cassidy p15, p27, p41, p91, p147; Jean Cazals p63, p71, p87, p95, p97, p109; Tim Evans Cook p81; Francine Lawrence p203; Lisa Linder p113; William Lingwood p33, p89, p177; David Munns p13, p21, p25, p39, p49, p65, p67, p93, p115, p123, p137, p165, p173, p179, p181, p183, p191; Myles New p209; Lis Parsons p107; Michael Paul p207; Craig Robertson p105, p161, p195; Roger Stowell p53, p69, p77, p103, p125, p131, p141, p151, p153, p155, p157, p159, p187; Simon Walton p189, p205; Martin Thompson p201; Cameron Watt p23, p61, p139, p169, p211; Philip Webb p11, p17, p29, p35, p51, p57, p59, p73, p75, p85, p133, p145, p149, p167, p171, p185, p193, p199; Simon Wheeler p55, p73, p79, p83, p101, p111, p129, p135; Jonathan Whittaker p127; Geoff Wilkinson p99; Tim Young p37.

All the recipes in this book have been created by the editorial team on *BBC Good Food Magazine*:

Lorna Brash, Sara Buenfeld, Mary Cadogan, Barney Desmazery, Jane Hornby, Emma Lewis, Kate Moseley, Orlando Murrin, Vicky Musselman, Angela Nilsen, Maggie Pannell, Jenny White, Jeni Wright.